Viva Italia

180 CLASSIC RECIPES

TOMAS TENGBY & ULRIKA TENGBY HOLM

TRANSLATED BY STINE OSTTVEIT

Skyhorse Publishing

Skyhorse Publishing books may be purchased in bulk at special discounts for sales promotion, corporate gifts, fund-raising, or educational purposes. Special editions can also be created to specifications. For details, contact the Special Sales Department, Skyhorse Publishing, 307 West 36th Street, 11th Floor, New York, NY 10018 or info@skyhorsepublishing.com.

Skyhorse® and Skyhorse Publishing® are registered trademarks of Skyhorse Publishing, Inc.®, a Delaware corporation.

Visit our website at www.skyhorsepublishing.com.

10 9 8 7 6 5 4 3 2 1

Library of Congress Cataloging-in-Publication Data is available on file.

ISBN: 978-1-61608-880-4

Printed in China

180 CLASSIC RECIPES

~ Contents ~

ANTIPASTI
Appetizers 18

PRIMI
Zuppe—soups 34
Pasta 46
Riso e polenta—rice and polenta 80

SECONDI
Carne e pollo—meat and chicken 92
Pesce—fish and shellfish 120

CONTORNI E VERDURE
Sides and vegetables 136

PANE E PIZZE
Bread and pizza 160

DOLCI
Desserts and sweets 172

All recipes serve four people unless otherwise specified.

GUEST COOKS

THIS IS THE BOOK WE'VE ALWAYS DREAMED OF WRITING.

For twenty years we have been traveling to Italy as often as possible, but far from as often as we might have wanted. We have rented houses and apartments and stayed in hotels. We have continually discovered new places and revisited the old and familiar ones. In a sense, we have always been preparing to write The Great Italian Cookbook.

Food has always been our main focus. This happens easily in Italy.

The fantastic ingredients. The wonderful flavors. All the ingenious, simple dishes.

We have eaten, enjoyed, and documented it all.

We have traveled around the north, through the Italian Alps, and seen Lake Como, Lake Garda, Verona, Venice. We have explored the cities of Tuscany: cultural and historical giants like Florence, Siena, and Volterra. The delicious food in charming Bologna. The great Rome that somehow still feels intimate. The sun, sea, mozzarella, and lemons of the Bay of Naples and the Amalfi Coast. Peaceful Sardinia with its distinct food and nature, and vast, friendly, hospitable Sicily, where a millennium's worth of history shows itself everywhere—in landscapes, in the architecture, and not least in the food.

THESE PLACES HAVE BECOME OUR FRIENDS. One learns to know them, to know their best sides, know their secrets, and know what to shy away from. They feel safe. They are welcoming and familiar. And even

We have eaten, enjoyed, and documented everything there is to try in Italy.

when you think you know them all too well, they'll suddenly surprise you with a new side of themselves.

Food plays a key role in our relationship with Italy, but everything is bound together. The people, their hospitality, their love of children, simplicity, effortlessness, the landscapes, art, culture, elegance, fashion—everything you could ever want!

Italians know how to make life enjoyable. *La dolce vita*, the sweet life. You don't have to live in Italy to experience it, but it certainly helps!

OVER THE COURSE OF THESE TWENTY YEARS, OUR relationship with Italian food has only grown stronger. And the more we've learned, the more apparent it's become that Italian food is mainly about three things: simplicity, clarity, and flavor. That's a combination that is hard to resist.

In Italy, people are locally "patriotic"; they are not Italian but rather Tuscan, Sicilian, or Piedmontese. If they meet someone from the same region, they will identify with their province, and then their town or city. No one is surprised if someone badmouths a food from another area. One's local cuisine is always the best.

As Swedes we didn't grow up with these traditions, preferences, and set points of view. Our advantage as non-Italians is that we can enjoy all of the great food of Italy without the interference of a regionally biased appetite; we can love dishes from North as well as South, because we don't have to be loyal to a certain heritage.

Simply put: We have worked to bring Italy to Sweden—and now to the US.

Sometimes dreams actually happen.

Ulrika and Tomas

Food Is life

Whether it's a weekday or the weekend, for an Italian, the meals are always the highlight of the day. In between, they talk about the food they have eaten and the food they will be eating. Because life should be enjoyed. A lovely meal with good food—something that is often reserved for holidays and other special occasions in other parts of Europe and the US—is nothing out of the ordinary in Italy. An Italian expects to eat good food for lunch and dinner all week long. It's also important to share the food with others and eat together—preferably with people you like.

We were in a small coastal town in the far south of Tuscany. In the harbor, right behind a small cozy trattoria, there is a tiny little beach. As we were enjoying the sun we couldn't help but overhear the conversation of a few Italians, a number of well-dressed ladies and a young man who had just arrived. He was saying that he had just come from Rome and that it was his first time visiting this place.

"And what do you eat here?" he asked.

"You should be very pleased that you came here," the women quickly responded, "because here you will find the best food."

"Oh, well, we all know that Rome has the best food," the man protested

These strangers continued to talk about food for twenty minutes.

The ladies described one delicious dish after the other. The man from Rome only agreed that it sounded interesting, though a tad bit different, and clearly not on par with the cuisine of the capital, which he went on to describe in detail.

That's Italy.

You talk about food.

"What did you eat today?" is a common way to open a conversation; the conversation will continue with, "And what will you eat later?" Italians will talk about the wonderful meals they have eaten and the ones they have yet to eat, and they'll discuss the lovely produce that's in season, or will be soon.

It's an American misconception that we must live to

work. Or, for that matter, that we must eat to live. Every Italian knows that food is life, and life is food.

FOOD IS A CORNERSTONE of human existence. Meals should be taken seriously (except maybe breakfast). There is always time for food. Everything else can wait.

"Food is the actual religion in Italy"—or so said the American detective novelist Donna Leon when we met her in Venice, where she has lived for thirty years. "Christianity is just a theatrical backdrop. Food is the true God. After all, it fulfills the same functions as religion: It gives its followers comfort, a sense of security, and common ground."

Of course, believers in different regional cuisines all agree that their god is the greatest. The Romans believe that Roman food reigns supreme, whereas Tuscans worship Tuscan cuisine, as if they were two totally different faiths without even the most basic tenets in common.

IN ORDER TO REALLY UNDERSTAND our little story we'll need to review Italian geography. The small coastal town where the story takes place is located in Tuscany, near the border with Lazio, where Rome is. So all in all the young man had traveled ninety miles—but for him it was like entering a different country with a different religion.

"Food is without a doubt one of the most important parts of life in Italy," Donna Leon concludes. "It's one the main reasons why it is so enjoyable to live here."

Of course one should enjoy food. Of course food should take time and cost money. What's appealing about the alternative? Where's the pleasure in eating quickly and cheaply? But then again, most Italians view life in general as something to be enjoyed. Everything in life should be as fun, attractive, and luxurious as possible.

"You only live once," our friend Chef Pietri Fiorinello, says to us. "Life is short, so why be careless with food?"

Nevertheless, life has changed in Italy. In the larger cities many people no longer eat two-hour-long lunches or leave work in the middle of the day to go home and eat with their families. A growing number of people eat a quick lunch while standing. But even if lunch is just a sandwich, it's still filled with the finest cold cuts and the best cheese.

The past decades of Italian food culture won't disappear in the blink of an eye.

You should never be careless when it comes to food.
There is always time for food.
Everything else can wait.

Food in Italian

The Italian eating schedule is organized in such a way that one is enjoying food or drink at virtually every time of day (in between one tries to squeeze in some work). To eat in the Italian fashion means eating smaller portions (a necessity, because otherwise you would never be able to eat it all). One must also allow every taste and ingredient to have its moment, which is why each component of a meal is served on a separate plate. Eating the Italian way also means taking your time; you need time to experience and enjoy everything, and you also need time to talk. Traditionally, the main meal is lunch, il pranzo, and this grand production's division into four acts—*antipasti*, *primi*, *secondi* and *dolci*—is also the way we have chosen to divide this book.

A Typical Day

BREAKFAST, COLAZIONE, IS AN IDEA THAT NEVER really caught on in Italy. At home, Italians drink a cup of coffee from an angular stovetop coffee brewer, sometimes with a little milk, and at most, a croissant or other pastry. A good breakfast for children, many commercials say, is warm milk and a handful of cookies.

Hunger soon returns, so most people will stop at their favorite coffee shop, or bar, on the way to work, where they might have a cappuccino, an Italian croissant, or *cornetto*, filled with vanilla cream, apricot jam, or chocolate, and a glass of freshly squeezed orange juice.

One might also eat a sandwich, or *panino*, with cold cuts, cheese, or a pickled vegetable—if not in the morning then at least by midday.

At some point between noon and three it is time for lunch, *pranzo*. Outside of the largest cities this is still the most important meal of the day and includes an *antipasto*, *primo*, *secondo*, and *dolce*. A traditional lunch can take up to two hours. Many people go home to eat. Children come home from school. Shops and offices close in the middle of the day and open again in the afternoon. People will even drive their cars from the cities out to trattorias in the countryside for a real four-course lunch.

IN THE LARGE CITIES, MANY LIVE a more hectic life and have adopted the strange American and Northern European habit of throwing something down quickly for lunch. For them, the evening meal is the big one, even

if it doesn't follow the traditional four-course structure. On Sundays, even these lost souls will gather their entire family together to eat a proper Italian lunch that goes on for several hours.

In the afternoon there should always at least be time for a visit to the *bar* for a quick espresso and a quick conversation on the sidewalk.

Since dinner, *cena*, will not be served until sometime between 7:30 and 10:00 at night, they might eat a snack before that as well. Many bars serve appetizers, *aperitivi*, *stuzzichini*, or *cicchetti*, or they may offer full buffets. A glass of wine and a couple of mouthfuls is the Italian version of happy hour.

If you've eaten a large lunch, dinner will be a more casual affair. Maybe just a pasta dish with a vegetable side or even a pizza at a restaurant. (Pizza is typically a dinner food, unless otherwise specified on signs: *pizza per pranzo*, pizza for lunch). Dessert is usually fresh fruit.

THE EVENING WALK, or *passeggiata*, is when you show yourself off and check out other people from every generation doing the same. This will entail another visit to the bar, where you'll order an espresso, maybe a piece of cake or pie for dessert, and an herb liqueur, *amaro*, for digestion. And then ice cream. *Gelato* and *sorbetto*, which is eaten on the sidewalk or while walking.

In short: Italians do everything they can to maximize their enjoyment. Every day.

The Meals of the Day

ANTIPASTI, the appetizers that lead into the actual meal, come first. There are often several antipasti, but care is taken to avoid mixing flavors. Each flavor, each ingredient, should be sampled at leisure before moving on to the next one. That is why there are often multiple small plates.

Primi piatti or *primi* are the dishes that make up the first course. Some examples of *primi* are soup, pasta, rice dishes, polenta, and gnocchi. Much of the food that has come to define Italy in the rest of the world falls into this category. In our part of the world, the first course is smaller than the main course, but this is not true for the *primo* and *secondo*, which are equally important and of equal size. In other words, the amount of food on your plate will not increase as the meal progresses. This surprises many restaurant-goers who are used to larger portions.

THE SECOND COURSE IS MADE UP OF THE *secondi piatti* or *secondi*, which consist of fish and shellfish, meat, poultry, and game. Simply prepared and served to bring out the best in each flavor. Once again, many foreign diners are surprised to receive a piece of meat and a lemon wedge—where is everything else? If you want some extras to accompany your meat dish, you have to order them as separate sides, *contorni*, which

means vegetables, *verdure*. These can be anything from a simple salad, to roasted potatoes, to a variety of other small vegetable dishes. As with the *antipasti*, different vegetables are rarely mixed together, so that each and every one gets to hold the spotlight.

Desserts, *dolci*, are not the stars of the Italian meal. The most important thing to have is fresh, sliced seasonal fruit. If the fruit isn't served on its own, they might make simple desserts in which the flavors of the fruits or berries are emphasized, though of course there is a wide array of classic desserts to choose from. If you still have room, restaurants will also offer rich cakes and pies.

BUT THIS DIVISION INTO CATEGORIES is not the law, and there are many variations. There are those who eat many *antipasti*, skip the *primo*, and move directly on to the *secondo*, those who go directly from pasta and to *dolci*, and there are those who have a pasta and then move on to fish, with our without a *contorno*. Waiters who protest only do so because they want to sell you more. Look at the Italians sitting at the table next to you and you will see that you can order as you please. Simply say "*Mi piace*"—I like it that way—and everything will be understood. (Everything, that is, except the habit of eating vegetables, meat, and pasta off of one plate. That is barbaric.)

Preparing Food the Italian way

IT'S NOT DIFFICULT TO COOK like an Italian. It's all about being attentive, both when buying ingredients and when preparing them.

Italians possess a vast knowledge of produce and other ingredients, and one never misses an opportunity to use something as much as possible when it is in season, which of course is the natural way to do things. Different ingredients and preparations are celebrated all over the country with special parties and festivals, *sagre*. One looks forward to the different seasons of the year, and when they've come and gone, one just has to accept that it will be a full year until next time.

Italians also know that ingredients will be at their freshest and ripest when they come from the area. Locally grown, *nostril*, or *nostrale*, is a strong selling point. The environmental benefits of eating locally have become a bonus for many, but first and foremost the habit of buying locally grown and produced foods is driven by a desire for flavor and quality.

But all this attention to ingredients will be for nothing if you are not attentive in the kitchen. While preparing the food, you need to be present and mindful of the process, following the different steps in due course and working to develop the flavors.

Making good food is less about recipes and more about knowing what to do to get the results you want. Methods will vary depending on the ingredients and the time one is willing to devote to cooking. Sometimes some sugar is needed to enhance the taste. Sometimes more basil, sometimes less.

MANY DISHES BEGIN WITH A SOFFRITTO.
Or rather, to start at the beginning: Many dishes begin with a *battuto* (after the verb *battere*, to punch and knock; also known as a *mirepoix* in French cuisine), a combination of finely chopped vegetables, usually yellow onion, carrot, and celery, and sometimes garlic, pancetta, or bacon. Later, when sautéed, it becomes a *soffritto*.

Depending on the recipe, you'll start with some olive oil, butter, or bacon in the pan. Then you'll move on to the yellow onion. The oil, butter, or fat should be hot enough that the onion is sautéed but not so hot that it browns. The onion should soften, lose its liquid, and take on a slightly golden color. This takes longer than you might think, but it is important because it brings the flavors out; the onion should become sweet. You can add some salt to the pan to help the onion along as it releases liquid. Be careful, though, because if the pan isn't hot enough, the onion will boil in its own liquid.

Yellow onion and garlic can be tricky to fry together because the garlic browns a lot quicker. There is a risk of the garlic burning, and then it will take on a bitter taste before the onion even starts to soften.

The best approach is to add the garlic when the yellow onion has achieved its flavor, and you can also lower the temperature a little to make sure that the garlic doesn't burn.

WHEN THE GARLIC STARTS TO SMELL IRRESISTIBLE and has some color, add the celery and sauté the same way, until soft, but without browning. Then add the carrots and sauté them until they are soft and sweet.

To allow the flavors of the various ingredients to develop and come together with everything else in the pan has a word in Italy: *insaporire*. This means to flavor, season, or add taste, and it is a term that requires no further explanation. It may seem tedious to prepare foods this way rather than frying everything at once, but it tastes better, and it is what makes the difference between a fantastic dish and a mediocre one.

If you lovingly work the *soffritto* the ingredients that are added later in the process will be *insaporiti*, absorbing the flavors already in the pan and releasing all of their flavors in turn. This is cooking according to the method 1+1+1=7; in other words, the flavors will significantly exceed your expectations.

It is impossible to say for sure how long this takes altogether, how many minutes one vegetable should be sautéed for, and how many minutes should be devoted to the others. It depends on the produce. If the ingredients are flavorful and sweet to begin with, the *soffritto* will come together very quickly. This is for you to figure out by being active and present while cooking, stirring to avoid burning and increasing or lowering the temperature as necessary. It's easy to keep the temperature too low out of fear of burning the food, so pay attention to how it smells and tastes.

If pancetta or bacon is included in the dish it should first be fried in some butter or olive oil until it releases some of its fat. Yellow onion can be added as soon as there is enough grease in the pan for it to sauté in. When meat is part of the dish, it is usually browned in olive oil or butter and then removed from the pan while the *soffritto* is cooked.

Risotto, *ragù*, seafood pasta, minestrone—many dishes are prepared in exactly the same way, and you will encounter this technique again and again in the recipes in this book.

If you have yellow onion, celery, and carrots in your kitchen, you are well on your way. Flat-leaf parsley is also a common ingredient, so always keep a large bunch of it in your home.

ITALIAN COOKING USES A LOT OF FRESH HERBS, especially basil, but only when it's in season—in other words, during the summer. Basil is cultivated year-round in greenhouses but it still tastes noticeably better during the summer months.

Fresh tomatoes should be ripe and flavorful. Plum tomatoes are usually best for cooking. Blanch and peel them the following way: Cut a small cross at the top of each tomato and place in boiling water. Let the tomatoes boil for a couple of minutes until you see the skin loosening around the cuts. Drain and hold under cold running water, then peel. Cut open, remove the seeds, and dice. A faster approach is to filet them: Quarter the tomatoes, remove the seeds, and press them flat against a cutting board with the skin facing down. Then press a sharp knife against the cutting board and move it sideways to remove the skin.

If you can't find fresh tomatoes, it's better to use quality canned or bottled ones. This is what they do in Italy as well. Whether you use whole, peeled, crushed, or pureed tomatoes or cherry tomatoes is really up to you. But there is a difference between different kinds of canned tomatoes, and there's a reason that some are more expensive than others. Go for quality!

ANTIPASTI *appetizers*

Antipasto means "before the meal" and not "before the pasta," even though it is often served before pasta.

In Italy it's common to begin meals with one or more of these small dishes, or even build a whole meal out of multiple *antipasti,* buffet-style. *Antipasti* are also served at bars in early evening with a glass of wine.

With many of these dishes, you can increase the portions to create a stand-alone meal. A few favorites served together can become dinner.

There is no strict division between *antipasti* and *verdure e contorni,* the sides that accompany meat or fish. Many of the appetizer dishes in this book can be served as sides, and many of the dishes you will find in the verdure section in the second half of the book can be served as antipasti. Even bread, *pizzette,* and larger pizzas cut into slices are sometimes served as *antipasti.*

On the facing page is one of the most beloved appetizers: *affettati misti,* or mixed cold cuts, shown here with bread, olives, cheeses, and preserved vegetables.

Crostini & bruschetta

Crostini have been eaten for a very long time on the Italian peninsula; there are recipes dating back to the 1500s. *Crostini*, which simply means "toasted bread," are enjoyed from North to South. They're at their most delicious when made with day-old country bread toasted in the oven at about 350 F (180 C). *Crostini* are not to be confused with *bruschette*, which are made from larger slices of bread.

Crostini di fegatini
Crostini with chicken livers, Tuscany

1 small onion
3 tbsp olive oil
½ lb (250 g) chicken liver
2 garlic cloves
1 tbsp fresh sage
3 tbsp white wine
Capers for garnish
Crostini

Finely chop the onion and sauté until soft (but without browning it) in olive oil. Remove the onion from the pan and increase the heat.

Prepare the chicken livers by cleaning, trimming, and chopping them, then sauté them in the oil. Mince the garlic and chop the sage, then lower the heat, add to the pan, and sauté.

Add wine and bring the contents of the pan to a boil. Turn off the heat, pour the liver mixture into a food processor, and puree until smooth. Spread on the toasted bread slices, garnish with the capers, and serve immediately.

Crostini di tonno
Crostini with tuna, Tuscany

1 can of tuna in oil
3 tbsp (50 g) butter
2 tbsp chopped yellow onion
2 tbsp chopped flat-leaf parsley
1 tbsp lemon juice
salt
black pepper

Drain the tuna. Use a fork to break it up in a bowl and mix until smooth. Add butter, onion, and parsley and mix. Season with salt, lemon juice, and freshly ground pepper.

Crostini di olive
Crostini with olive pâté, Umbria

2 tbsp capers
4 anchovy filets
1–2 garlic cloves
5 oz (150 g) black olives, pitted
2 tbsp rum or cognac (optional)
5 tbsp olive oil

Rinse the capers. Rinse and dry the anchovies.

Peel the garlic cloves. Place everything in a food processor and pulse several times. Do not purée completely; the mixture should be a bit chunky.

Crostini di avocado e parmigiano
Crostini with avocado and Parmesan

1 ripe avocado
1 tsp lemon juice
3 tbsp freshly grated Parmesan
2 tbsp olive oil
black pepper

Scoop out the avocado. Cut into smaller pieces and place in a bowl. Add the lemon juice and blend together. Add the Parmesan and olive oil. Mash everything together with a fork until creamy. Season with freshly ground black pepper.

Bruschette
Toasted bread, Tuscany

The simplest form of *bruschetta* is a toasted slice of bread sprinkled with olive oil. In Tuscany this is also known as *fettunta*.

The next step up is to take that toasted slice of bread and rub it with garlic while still hot and then drizzle with olive oil. If you go on to add ripe tomatoes (deseeded and chopped), fresh basil, and some olive oil on top, you end up with one of the most common varieties, *bruschetta al pomodoro*.

Bruschetta ai funghi
Bruschetta with mushrooms

14 oz (400 g) assorted mushrooms
2 tbsp olive oil
Salt
Black pepper
2 garlic cloves
1 tbsp fresh thyme or 1 tsp dried

If the mushrooms are large, cut them into smaller pieces. Sauté in olive oil. Season with salt and pepper.

Add crushed garlic and chopped thyme and let everything sauté for a few minutes until the liquid from the mushrooms has evaporated.

Insalata caprese con rucola
Arugula, tomato, and mozzarella salad

A classic *insalata caprese*—literally, salad from Capri—is a summer dish prepared with fresh tomatoes, fresh basil, fresh mozzarella, salt, freshly ground black pepper, and olive oil.

The nicer and more flavorful buffalo mozzarella that is often served in this salad today wasn't originally part of the dish; rather, it was made with the more common cow's milk mozzarella from Sorrento, the closest city to Capri. This cheese is not actually called *mozzarella*, but rather *fior de latte*. Mozzarella technically only refers to the buffalo milk cheese, but because the names are so often confused, the cow's milk cheese has come to be known as *mozzarella* as well.

In this recipe, peppery arugula takes the place of basil, giving the dish more character. You should only ever make a *caprese* when you have access to exceptionally fine and ripe tomatoes—in other words, in the summertime.

3.5 oz (100 g) arugula, preferably wild
7 oz (200 g) tomatoes
5 oz (150 g) mozzarella, preferably mozzarella di bufala
coarse salt
black pepper

olive oil
or
dressing:
4 tbsp olive oil
1 tbsp white wine vinegar
½ tsp sugar or honey

Rinse and dry the arugula. Slice the tomatoes and mozzarella. Place everything in a bowl, sprinkle with salt, and grind pepper on top.

Drizzle with olive oil or blend the dressing with olive oil, white wine vinegar, and some sugar or honey and drizzle over the salad. Toss everything together and serve.

Insalate di arance
Orange salad, Sicily

One of the greatest joys of winter are the delicious citrus fruits that come into season during the colder months, especially Sicilian blood oranges, which turn up right before Christmas and can be found for the two following months. For more on blood oranges, see the recipe for blood orange sorbet on page 188.

Both fennel and olives work well with oranges; salt and olive oil elevate the flavors even more. Even a regular mixed green salad will reach new heights when oranges are added.

Insalata di arance rosse
Blood orange salad

Blood oranges
Black olives, preferably Italian, such as the smaller taggiasca variety, commonly known as niçoise
Black pepper
Olive oil
Fresh mint
Salt

Peel the oranges and remove the pith. Slice thinly. Blood oranges usually do not have seeds, but if they do, remove them. Remember to save the juice as well. Arrange the slices on plates.

Arrange the olives among the orange slices. Add a few grinds from a peppermill. Drizzle with the orange juice and a generous amount of olive oil. You may also add a few mint leaves if desired.

The olives will make the salad salty, but if you wish you may also add salt to taste.

Insalata di arance e finocchio
Orange and fennel salad

A few juicy oranges
1 fennel bulb
1 small red onion
Radishes (optional)
Black olives (optional)
Fresh mint (optional)
Black pepper
Salt
Olive oil

Remove the stalks from the fennel, set the fennel fronds aside, and remove any inedible parts of the fennel. Slice it down the middle and then once in the opposite direction so that you are left with four pieces. Remove as much as possible of the hard root in the middle. Cut the fennel into thin slices, preferably using a mandolin.

Peel the onion and cut it into thin slices. If you are using radishes, slice these as well.

Peel the oranges and remove the pith. Cut into thin slices. Remove the seeds. Save the juice.

Arrange the fennel on plates and then place the orange slices, red onion, radishes, and olives on top. Top this with a shredded mint leaf. Pour the orange juice over the salad.

Add black pepper from a few turns of the peppermill and season with salt. Drizzle with a generous amount of olive oil and decorate with the fennel fronds.

Bagna Cauda
Raw vegetables in warm anchovy sauce, Piedmont

In the local dialect, *bagna caôda* means "hot bath." The dish is believed to have originated with Piedmontese winemakers.

Traditionally, the sauce is prepared in a terracotta bowl, and the ingredients are cooked over low heat and stirred until they melt and the sauce becomes smooth. Sometimes white truffle oil is added for flavor. The sauce is kept warm, heated either by candle or on a fondue warmer, and is used as a dipping sauce for raw vegetables.

You can also use it as a dipping sauce for lightly boiled vegetables, like onions, or ones that have been completely boiled, like potatoes.

If you start to run low on the sauce you can add some olive oil. The last tablespoons of sauce may be added to a couple of scrambled eggs for an extra treat.

Raw vegetables are served in similar ways in other parts of Italy as well. During the summer months it is common to dip raw vegetables in a quality olive oil that has been seasoned with salt and black pepper and perhaps some vinegar as well. This is known as *pinzimonio*, possibly because your fingers resemble pincers when you are holding the vegetables.

3.5 oz (100g) preserved anchovy filets
4–6 garlic wedges
3 tbsp (50 g) butter
1 cup (2 dl) olive oil

a good country bread

cauliflower
broccoli
endive
fennel
Jerusalem artichoke
celery
bell peppers (different colors)
carrots
scallions
mushrooms

Begin by soaking the vegetables in cold water for a while. (This makes them crisper.)

Rinse, dry, and mince the anchovy filets. Mince the garlic as well.

Melt the butter over low heat, preferably using a water bath. Add the garlic and heat carefully until it is soft but not browned. It should be so soft that it is almost dissolving.

Add the anchovy bits and some of the olive oil, keeping the heat low and stirring until the anchovies have dissolved. Add the rest of the olive oil and heat until warm.

Rinse, dry, and cut the vegetables into sticks or smaller pieces. If you wish to boil a vegetable, run it under cold water afterwards so that it cools, and then dry it off.

Arrange all of the vegetables on a large platter and place on the table, along with the bread and the warm sauce.

Insalata di farro
Spelt salad, Tuscany

Farro is the Italian word for the traditional wheat variety we call spelt or dinkel. The original wheat arrived in the Mediterranean by way of the Middle East, and in Roman times it was the most important food on the Italian peninsula.

Spelt has a somewhat nutty flavor and is perfect in salad and in soups. Moreover, it is very healthy and a good alternative for those who cannot eat regular wheat.

1 cup (2 dl) farro (spelt, dinkel, or similar wheat berries)
4–6 radishes
2 tomatoes
½ cucumber
2 handfuls of pitted black olives
A generous amount of fresh basil
3 tbsp olive oil
salt
black pepper
lettuce leaves
4 hardboiled eggs
lemon juice

Boil the wheat berries in salted water as instructed on the package. Drain and let cool.

Cut the radishes into thin slices. Dice the tomatoes and the cucumber (you should use approximately the same amount of each). Cut up the basil.

Combine the wheat berries with the radishes, tomatoes, cucumber, basil, and olives. Drizzle with olive oil and add salt and freshly ground pepper.

Rinse and dry the lettuce leaves. Arrange them on plates and scoop the wheat salad on top. Quarter the eggs and place them on top. Drizzle with lemon juice.

Prosciutto e fichi
Prosciutto with figs, Friuli-Venezia Giulia

Mild figs with mild ham. You can also serve figs with spicier salami; in that case the sweetness of the fig will be more prevalent. Handle the figs carefully as they are sensitive to impact.

Figs are very flavorful when ripe, but they have almost no taste at all when they are unripe. Ripe figs go bad quickly, so be sure to eat them right away.

8 fresh, ripe figs
5 oz (150 g) prosciutto crudo, for instance prosciutto di San
   Daniele or prosciutto di Parma
Black pepper

Cut the figs into four wedges each. Arrange the figs on plates with the prosciutto on top. If you want, you can top it off with some freshly ground pepper. Serve with bread.

Pomodori alla marsalese
Tomatoes stuffed with shrimp, Sicily

This is a dish from Marsala, a coastal town south of Trapani in western Sicily. The name derives from Arabic and may have originally meant either *Marsa Ali*, Ali's port (Ali also means great) or *Marsa Allah*, Allah's port

Wine and olives are widely cultivated in this area. There are also many salt ponds where sea salt is harvested (see the picture on page 134)

The famous Marsala Wine is made in the same manner as sherry or port and is of British origin.

The tomatoes used in this dish should be large, firm, and, of course, ripe and flavorful. Cooked shrimp are often salty enough, but if you make the dish with raw shrimp, you may need to add salt.

4 large tomatoes
1 lb 10 oz (750 g) unpeeled boiled shrimp or ½ lb (250 g)
peeled
½ lb (250 g) pitted green olives
2 anchovy filets
3 tbsp olive oil
1 tbsp lemon juice
chili flakes, enough to equal ½ a small peperoncino
black pepper
flat-leaf parsley

Preheat the oven to 440 F (225 C) degrees.

Cut off the tops of the tomatoes. Scoop the insides out with a spoon without breaking the walls of the tomatoes.

Thaw and peel the shrimp.

Chop the olives. There should be roughly the same amount of shrimps and olives.

Rinse, dry, and finely chop the anchovies.

Mix shrimp, anchovies, olives, olive oil, and lemon juice together in a bowl. Season with the chili flakes and freshly ground black pepper. Stuff the tomatoes with the mixture. Place on a baking sheet and roast in the oven until the tomatoes have some color, about 15 minutes.

Garnish with parsley and serve warm.

Pomodori al tonno
Tomatoes with tuna, Sicily

4 large tomatoes
1 small yellow onion
olive oil
1 garlic clove
1 can of tuna fish in oil
bread crumbs
2 tbsp capers
¼ cup (½ dl) chopped pitted black olives
flat-leaf parsley
Parmesan

Preheat the oven to 440 F (225 C) degrees.

Cut the top off of each tomato right below the calyx.

Scoop the insides out with a spoon without damaging the walls of the tomatoes.

Finely chop the onion and sauté in olive oil so that it softens but does not brown. Mince the garlic and sauté that as well, also without browning.

Drain the tuna and cut into smaller pieces. Let the tuna and bread crumbs sauté with the onion and garlic for a couple of minutes. Remove from the stove. Add capers, olives, and chopped parsley.

Stuff the tomatoes with the mixture. Top it off with grated Parmesan. Place the tomatoes on a baking sheet and let them roast in the oven for 15–20 minutes. Serve warm.

Vitello tonnato
Veal with tuna sauce, Piedmont

At restaurants, one is often served a couple of slices of boiled veal with a mayonnaise sauce drizzled on top. This is good, but it tastes even better when you arrange the veal slices and sauce in layers and let the dish rest for a while, even overnight, in the fridge. This really brings out the flavors and gives them a chance to blend, although it might not look as pretty. In Milan they also do a warm version of this dish.

1.3–1.5 lb (600–700 g) veal
1 celery stalk
1 yellow onion
1 carrot
1 bay leaf
water

Trim the veal into a shape resembling a slightly elongated rectangle and truss it with string, or buy a piece of meat that is already trussed.

Place in a heavy pot with celery, onion, carrot, and the bay leaf and cook until tender, for about 1 hour. Let cool in the broth. Set the broth aside.

Remove the string or net. Cut into thin slices.

Mayonnaise sauce:
1 yolk
1 tbsp lemon juice or white wine vinegar
½–¾ cup (1 ½ dl) olive oil
a pinch of salt

Make sure that the yolk and oil are the same temperature.

Place the yolk and lemon juice or vinegar in a bowl. Slowly add the oil while whisking. Once the blend has thickened you can add the remaining oil and whisk to blend. Season with salt.

Sauce:
½ can tuna (1 can 7 oz (200 g) net weight)
2 ½ anchovy filets
½ cup (1 ¼ dl) olive oil
1 ½ tbsp lemon juice
1 ½ tbsp capers

Puree tuna, anchovies, olive oil, lemon juice, and capers in a blender or food processor until smooth. Stir in the mayonnaise. Dilute the sauce with the broth from the meat. The sauce should not be too thick.

Spread some sauce on a serving plate. Cover with a layer of veal slices. Add another layer of sauce and follow with the veal.

Cover the plate with plastic wrap and place in the fridge. You can keep it there for several days, but be sure to refrigerate it for at least a couple of hours before serving.

Garnish with capers and lemon slices prior to serving.

with the white sauce drizzled on top. Today, however, the dish is often served with arugula, olive oil, lemon, and Parmesan instead. An expensive meat slicer is needed to cut the slices thin enough, but somewhat thicker slices cut by hand are just as delicious.

Ultimately, the quality of the meat is the most important factor.

7 oz (200 g) beef tenderloin
arugula
0.8 oz (25 g) Parmesan
salt flakes
juice of 1 lemon
olive oil

Trim the fat off of the meat, wrap it in plastic wrap, and freeze it for 2 hours. Cut into thin slices. It will be easier to slice the meat once it's been frozen.

Let the slices return to room temperature, then arrange them on plates. Rinse, dry, and arrange the arugula on top.

Use a potato peeler to shave off thin flakes of Parmesan.

Add the shaved Parmesan to the plate, sprinkle with salt, and squeeze lemon juice on top. Top it off with olive oil.

Mayonnaise sauce:
1 yolk
½ tbsp lemon juice
½ cup (1 dl) neutral-tasting oil (canola or corn oil)
1 tbsp lemon juice or white wine vinegar
1 ½ tbsp milk
½ tbsp Worchester sauce
salt
black
Mustard powder or Dijon mustard (optional)

Make sure that the egg and the yolk are the same temperature.

Place the yolk and lemon juice or vinegar in a bowl. Carefully add the oil while whisking constantly. After the blend has thickened you no longer have to be as careful with the oil. Add milk and Worchester sauce, additional lemon juice, salt, freshly ground black pepper, and some mustard if desired.

Drizzle the sauce on top of the Carpaccio.

Carpaccio
Veneto

These days, *carpaccio* is made from many different ingredients and is essentially understood as "thin slices" of raw meat or fish. The original, however, was made from beef. The idea of serving raw meat can't be accredited to anyone in particular, but *carpaccio* originated at Harry's Bar in Venice.

Amalia Nani Mocenigo, a regular patron and a member of the Venetian aristocracy, was following a protein diet and in 1949 the owner of the bar, Giuseppe Cipriani, served her raw meat with a special sauce made with mayonnaise, Worchester sauce, mustard, and milk.

The dish was called "steak with universal sauce" but was renamed the following year. In 1950, there was a large exhibit in Venice of paintings by the local Renaissance painter Vittore Carpaccio. Cipriani associated the red and white colors of the dish with the color choices of Carpaccio.

A traditional *carpaccio* consists of thin slices of meat

Suppli al telefono
Fried riceballs, Lazio

These Roman-style riceballs are filled with mozzarella, and when you take a bite the melted cheese stretches into long threads like telephone wires, hence the name. *Suppli* may be a dialectal variation on the word *sorpresa*, surprise. This would make sense because the filling varies, so you never really know what you're going to get. They can be stuffed with mushrooms, chicken, ham, and so on.

Riceballs can be made with leftover risotto, but it can't be too runny or you will have to add eggs. Leftovers like ragú or chicken can also be used as fillings.

10 oz (300 g) rice
salt
1 ½ tbsp (25 g) butter
2 tbsp grated Parmesan
4.5 oz (125 g) diced mozzarella
2 eggs
bread crumbs
oil for frying

Boil the rice in a generous amount of salted water. Pour the water off. Place the rice in a bowl and mix with butter and Parmesan. Spread the rice out on a baking sheet or a countertop covered in parchment paper so that it cools faster. Shape the rice into small balls. Poke a hole in each ball, push one of the mozzarella cubes inside, and close up the hole.

Whisk the eggs in a bowl. Pour the breadcrumbs out on a separate plate. Dip the buns in the egg and dredge them in the breadcrumbs. Pat the breadcrumbs in place so that they stick. Set the riceballs aside and allow to dry.

Heat frying oil in a frying pan or saucepan to 350 F (180 C). (This is the temperature at which a small piece of bread will brown in about 30 seconds, though you can get a more accurate reading with a thermometer.) Fry the riceballs until they have a nice golden color. Let them drain on some paper towels and serve immediately.

Arancini

Arancini—literally, "small oranges"—are the Sicilian variety of fried riceballs. They are often stuffed with ground meat sauce, with green peas and mozzarella, or *caciocavallo* (see page 220) and flavored with saffron, which is added to either the rice or the ground meat.

Ground meat sauce for Arancini:

½ cup (1 dl) frozen peas
3.5 oz (100g) ground meat
olive oil
½ garlic clove and/or 2 tbsp finely chopped yellow onion
½ cup (1 dl) dry white wine
saffron (optional)
2 tbsp tomato puree
salt
black pepper

Thaw the peas. Fry the ground meat in olive oil. Lower the heat and add the half crushed garlic clove and/or yellow onion and sauté until soft. Add the wine and bring the mixture to a boil. Add some saffron if desired. Add tomato puree, stir, and let simmer, covered, for about 20 minutes. Season with salt and freshly ground black pepper. Let cool.

Make the riceballs the same way as in the previous recipe for *suppli* al telefono. Push some of the filling and cheese into the middle of the balls and then close up the hole by covering it with some of the rice. Bread and fry the same way as *suppli*.

Frittata

A *frittata* is a *frittata* and not an omelet or a tortilla. It may be eaten warm or cold, as an appetizer, as a light lunch with a salad, or as a snack with a glass of wine in early evening when dinner is still an hour away. We recommend using a smaller pan so that the frittata will be deeper.

Frittate are most often cooked all the way through, so they are not runny the way French omelets are. This way, they taste better cold. Either they are cooked all the way through on the stovetop without being flipped, or it is cooked in the oven for a firmer surface. A *frittata* can also be flipped with the aid of a plate. To do this, place the plate over the pan, carefully turn the pan upside down and transfer the frittata to the plate, and slide it back into the pan with the opposite side facing down.

Feel free to make multiple *frittate* with various fillings; they are very quick to make and they're delicious to boot. You can use pretty much anything as a filling or to add flavor. Try quartered artichokes. (Fresh artichokes are fried and then boiled, covered. Preserved artichokes are quicker.) Or try asparagus and some Parmesan. Or zucchini and basil. Or you can use some onions (sautéed until soft, without browning) and lots of arugula. Or simply use lots of fresh herbs. Or garlic and mushroom. Or thinly sliced potatoes, fried, with bell peppers, and maybe some boiled ham or prosciutto di Parma.

There will usually be some cheese in the *frittata* as well: Parmesan, Pecorino, mozzarella, or Fontina, depending on what you have available.

Frittata ai pomodorini e basilico
Frittata with cherry tomatoes and basil, Campania

12 cherry tomatoes
olive oil
salt
black pepper
3 eggs
½ portion of mozzarella (about 2 oz (60 g))
1 handful basil leaves

Quarter the tomatoes. Heat oil in a pan. Sauté the tomatoes on high heat for a couple of minutes so that they release their water. Season with salt and ground black pepper.

Whisk the eggs in a bowl. Stir in diced mozzarella and shredded basil leaves. Lower to medium heat and add the mixture to the pan. Let it cook on the stovetop or in the oven, depending on which method you prefer, until it has cooked through and is ready to serve.

Frittata agli spaghetti
Frittata with spaghetti, Campania

Even though spaghetti is in the name of this dish, you can use other kinds of pasta too, making this a good way to put leftover pasta to use (and it tastes great without the ham or salami as well). If you decide that you want to give it a little extra bite, let the peperoncino and perhaps also a garlic clove brown with the oil in the beginning. This frittata looks like a beautiful golden tart. It will be even more beautiful if you flip it with a plate and fry it on both sides.

3 eggs
½ cup (1 dl) freshly grated pecorino or Parmesan
salt
black pepper
about 3.5 oz (100g) salami, boiled ham, or Parma ham
about 7 oz (200 g) cooked pasta such as spaghetti or linguine
olive oil
1 portion (4.5 oz / 125 g) mozzarella

Lightly whisk eggs, grated cheese, salt, and black pepper together in a bowl. Cut salami or ham into small pieces and add to the bowl along with the pasta.

Heat the olive oil in a medium pan. Pour in half of the egg mixture and spread it around evenly in the pan. Slice or dice the mozzarella and place on top of the eggs in the pan, avoiding the edges.

Cover with the rest of the egg mixture. Press down with the spatula to shape it so that it resembles a cake. Lower the heat and let it cook slowly, pressing down with the spatula as needed. Flip and fry on the opposite side. It will take about 15–20 minutes for the frittata to cook all the way through to a point where the spaghetti is kept in place by the eggs.

ZUPPE *Soups*

Soup is served as *primo piatto* after the *antipasto*.

A very rich soup can also be served as an entire meal on its own.

In Italian there are two words for soup: *zuppa* and *minestra*. The distinction between the two is unclear and varies from region to region. As a general rule, *zuppa* is thicker and almost like a stew, and should be served with bread rather than pasta or rice. *Minestra* is commonly a broth-based soup made with rice or pasta. A particularly rich *minestra* is called a *minestrone,* which means a large *minestra*. Conversely, a *minestrina* is a light soup with clear broth. *Brodo* means broth, but it can also refer to a thin soup. *Brodo ristretto* or just *ristretto* is a thin, clear soup.

Soups are made with inexpensive ingredients and lots of vegetables. Beans, for instance, are very common soup ingredients in every part of the country because they were traditionally a cheap source of protein. Old bread is also commonly used. Leftover dried pasta is put aside and saved in jars for use in soups.

Olive oil is often drizzled over soup before serving. Grated pecorino and Parmesan are also frequent additions.

Minestra di farro
Spelt soup, Molise

Farro was the wheat, spelt, or dinkel that served as a staple food in Roman times. When regular wheat came to replace *farro* in bread baking, *farro* continued to be used in soups.

There are various types of wheat products to choose from; you don't necessarily have to use spelt. Variations on *farro* soup can be found in the eastern regions Marche, Abruzzo, and Molise, but also in Umbria and Tuscany. The following is a delicious and flavorful variety that may be prepared in several ways. Leave out the pancetta or bacon and use a vegetable bouillon for a tasty vegetarian soup. If you wish, you may season your soup with fresh marjoram and/or basil, or serve it with freshly grated pecorino or Parmesan. Beans also make an excellent addition.

1.7 oz (50 g) pancetta or bacon
2 tbsp olive oil
1 yellow onion
1–2 small dried peperoncini, depending on potency
1 garlic clove
1 celery stalk
1 carrot
4 cups (1 liter) chicken stock
3–4 fresh tomatoes or 1 can (14 oz / 400 g) quality
*   tomatoes, without juice*
7 oz (200 g) (1 ¼–1 ½ cup / 2 ½–3 dl) wheat berries
salt
black pepper

Finely chop pancetta or bacon and fry in olive oil until it releases some of its fat, but do not brown.

Finely chop yellow onion and sauté until soft, but do not brown. Add the 1–2 peperoncini and sauté those with the onion. Use whole pepperoncini if you wish to remove them when the soup is ready.

Crush the garlic clove and add to the pot, sautéing without browning it. Finely chop celery, add to the pot, and sauté until soft. Peel and finely chop the carrot and sauté until soft as well.

Blanch, peel, seed, and dice the tomatoes. Add to the pan and sauté while stirring. Pour in the stock

and let the mixture come to a boil. Add the wheat berries. Cover and let simmer for 30 minutes. Season with salt and freshly ground pepper. Drizzle some olive oil on top before serving.

Minestra di orzo
Barley soup, Trentino–Alto Adige

Many variations on barley soup exist in the north of Italy, and it's no wonder considering the rich flavor that barley brings to the dish and how delightfully filling it is. In place of barley you can also use so-called barley rice, which is cut and pre-boiled barely that you only cook for about 8 minutes. But don't cut short the cooking time for the soup itself. It is only through slow cooking that the warming, buttery flavors of this soup come forth.

3 oz (80 g) trimmed bacon
1 yellow onion
2 stalks of celery
2 carrots
2 potatoes
1 small leek
2 tbsp olive oil
2 garlic cloves
7 oz (200 g) (2 ½ cup / 5 dl) barley
1 bay leaf
8 cups (2 liters) veal or beef stock
salt
black pepper
flat-leaf parsley

Cut the bacon into small pieces. Chop the yellow onion. Finely dice the celery. Peel and dice carrots and potatoes. Cut the leek in half lengthwise, rinse, and chop.

Fry the bacon in a pot until it releases its fat but do not let it brown. Add the onion and sauté until soft.

Crush the garlic cloves and add them to the pot, lowering the heat a little. Add the celery and let it sauté for a couple of minutes, then add the carrots and sauté for a couple of minutes more. Add the potatoes and sauté briefly, stirring constantly, as they stick easily.

Add barley, bay leaf, and the veal or beef stock. Cover and let simmer for 35–40 minutes. Season with salt and freshly ground pepper and garnish with chopped parsley.

Minestra di ceci

Chickpea soup, Sardinia

10.5 oz (300 g) dried chickpeas or 2 cans precooked
  canned chickpeas
1.7 oz (50 g) trimmed bacon
1 yellow onion
4 celery stalks
2 carrots
1 bunch flat-leaf parsley
3 tbsp olive oil
2 garlic cloves
2 tbsp tomato puree
8 cups (2 liters) beef or other meat stock
salt
black pepper

Soak dried chickpeas in water for about 10 hours.
(They should be well covered, so use twice as much
water as you have chickpeas.) Drain.

Cut the bacon into small pieces. Finely chop the onion. Slice
or dice the celery and carrots. Chop half of the parsley.

In a large pot or Dutch oven, fry the bacon in olive oil
until it releases its fat, but do not let it brown. Sauté the
onion until soft, again without browning. Crush the garlic cloves and add to the pot. Sauté the celery and then
the carrots. Add the chopped parsley. If using dried
chickpeas, stir in the tomato puree at this point and let
everything simmer for 5–7 minutes. (If using precooked
chickpeas, see below.)

Add the chickpeas and stock and bring the mixture to
a boil. Reduce the heat, cover, and let simmer until the
chickpeas are soft, about 1 hour. Season with salt and
freshly ground black pepper.

Chop the remaining parsley and sprinkle on top before
serving. Country bread is great as a side, preferably toasted.

If using boiled chickpeas you can add them when everything else has been sautéed. In this case, the soup will
only need to simmer for 20 minutes instead of 1 hour.

Pappa al pomodoro
Thick tomato soup, Tuscany

Pappa means gruel, porridge, or mush. This is a wonderful dish in the summer, when you can get a hold of really nice ripe and flavorful tomatoes. If not, it's best to use a high-quality canned tomato, or *polpa di pomodoro*.

The soup is wonderfully tart and sweet at the same time. You might want to add some sugar to enhance the flavors. The idea that you should never waste food is deeply rooted in Italian food culture, hence the many Italian soups like this one featuring stale bread. Old bread is an excellent ingredient and plays an important role in many Tuscan specialties.

4 thick slices of day-old country bread
3 garlic cloves
1 handful of basil leaves
5 tbsp olive oil
1 lb 10 oz (750 g) fresh tomatoes or 1–1.3 lb (500–600 g)
  polpa di pomodoro
chicken stock
salt
black pepper

Make sure that the bread you are using is dry and stale. If it is still soft then dry it in the oven on low heat for a few minutes, avoiding toasting it.

Mince the garlic. Cut the basil into small pieces. In a large pot, sauté the garlic and basil in olive oil until the garlic is soft but not browned.

Tear the bread into small pieces and add to the pot along with the tomatoes. Simmer for about 20 minutes, stirring occasionally. Add the chicken stock. The soup should be thick. Season with salt and freshly ground black pepper.

Shred some basil leaves and add them to the soup after ladling it into bowls. As a finishing touch, drizzle a thin line of olive oil on top.

This soup can be refrigerated and stored for a while without going bad. Just add some chicken stock or water before reheating to achieve the right texture.

VERONICA FAE FALDT IS PROUD of her Italian heritage.

"This shop is my dream. And my father's. He chose to do this and now he does it through me."

Pasquale Fae came to Sweden in the mid-1960s. He had already moved from his home island of Sardinia for a job at Fiat in Turin. Then Swedish ball bearing company SKF offered him a job, which took the young Italian to Gothenburg. He returned to Italy a couple of years later, as Gothenburg did not work out as he had hoped.

"But my father had met my mother at a dance at Rondo at Liseberg, and soon he was back in Gothenburg, giving it a second chance."

Pasquele married Anita, and in 1973, Veronica was born.

MANY ITALIANS LIVING IN SWEDEN struggled with the lack of really good food and in an effort to improve their quality of life took matters into their own hands. They ordered ingredients from back home and anyone who went to Italy for a visit always returned to Sweden with as many food products as possible. Suddenly there were Italian sausages and ham in Sweden (even though many of these were seized in customs). Some Italians left their factory jobs to start successful Italian restaurants.

"My father thought about it," Veronica says, "but chose his family."

PASQUELE IS FROM BENETUTTI, a city right in the middle of northern Sardinia with a few thousand inhabitants, a lot of history, thermal springs, and a shortage of jobs. When Veronica was a child the family traveled to Sardinia every summer in a little yellow Fiat in order to see family, hang out, and eat. Nowadays, they do this several times a year.

"There are large shared dinners, roast sucking pigs, and my father cooking. He's always enjoyed cooking."

"We eat Italian food regularly," Veronica says. "Simple, quick, with quality ingredients."

Veronica had a Catholic upbringing, and her own children are now learning Italian through home schooling.

"Of course we think about moving there. We'll see!"

La favata con pane carasau
Broad bean and sausage stew with Sardinian flatbread, Sardinia

"My grandmother used to make this in summertime," Veronica tells us. "It's rustic and delicious. She would use whatever was growing in her garden and I still remember how she shelled the beans."

Ideally, you should use *finocchietto selvatico*, wild fennel, instead of the cultivated variety. Dried beans have to be soaked overnight, so plan ahead. You can find frozen beans in Asian specialty shops. Remove the outer shell to reveal the light green bean within.

10.5 oz (300 g) Italian sausage
1 yellow onion
4 tbsp olive oil
2 garlic cloves
3 oz (80 g) pancetta
4 cups (1 L) beef stock
10.5 oz (300 g) fennel
14 oz (400 g) Savoy cabbage
12–16 cherry tomatoes
1.5 lb (600 g) frozen or dried
   broad beans, also known as
   fava beans
pecorino
flat-leaf parsley

Cut open the sausage and chop the yellow onion. Sauté the onion in a Dutch oven or stockpot with olive oil until it softens, being careful not to brown it. Add minced garlic and thinly sliced and shredded pancetta. Add 3 cups (6 dl) stock and let simmer for 10 minutes.

Shred the fennel and Savoy cabbage and add to the pot. Add the remaining stock. Simmer, covered, for 20–25 minutes.

Halve the tomatoes and add them along with the beans. Let the beans boil until they are al dente. Add shaved pecorino and chopped parsley to each bowl before serving. Eat with fried *pane carasau*, a Sardinian bread, if available.

Pane carasau is baked all over Sardinia, and you can usually find it in Italian specialty stores. It is crispy and should be eaten as is, added to salads, or soaked and added to soups and other dishes. It can also be fried briefly in sunflower oil to make *pane frattau*. Sprinkle this with salt flakes and your favorite fresh herbs after frying.

Veronica runs her family's specialty food shop, Delitalia, with her husband, Goran. The retired Pasquale stops by every day and makes sure that everything is in order. The last name Fae is a dialect word for fava, meaning broad bean. The name is pronounced FAH-uh, like fava, but without the "v."

Add the broccoli and let it sauté, stirring more or less constantly for a couple of minutes. Add some wine if using and bring to a simmer.

Pour in warm stock and bring to a boil. Add the pasta and cook until just al dente. Season with salt and pepper. Finally, add some lemon juice.

Top with chopped parsley and serve with freshly grated pecorino or Parmesan.

Minestra di broccoli
Broccoli soup, Lazio

For this soup we recommend using regular broccoli or Romanesco, which is popular in Rome and is a cross between broccoli and cabbage and has a mild cabbage taste. Use whatever kind of pork you have lying around. You can add some peperoncino for an extra kick.

1 lb (500 g) broccoli or Romanesco
1.7 oz (50 g) pancetta, bacon, or trimmed pork belly
2 plum tomatoes or ½ cup (1 dl) tomato puree or passata
2 garlic cloves and/or ½ small yellow onion
olive oil
a splash of dry white wine (optional)
vegetable or chicken stock
5 oz (150 g) spaghetti or other thin pasta
salt
black pepper
2 tsp lemon juice
flat-leaf parsley
pecorino Romano or Parmesan

Rinse the broccoli under cold water and cut off the florets, then divide the florets into smaller pieces.

Shred the pancetta, bacon, or pork belly. Blanch, peel, seed, and dice the tomatoes. Finely chop the garlic and/or yellow onion.

Fry the bacon until it releases its fat, but do not brown it. If you are using yellow onion, sauté it until soft, but do not let it brown. Add the garlic and sauté, taking care to avoid browning it as well.

Risi e bisi
Rice with peas, Veneto

This is a popular spring dish in Venice made with the fresh peas of the season. It used to be served on St. Mark's Day, April 25, to the *doge* of Venice, which was the city-state's highest office until the end of the eighteenth century. Risi e Bisi is Venetian for rice and peas. It's called *minestra*, soup, but it's actually a cross between soup and risotto. If fresh peas aren't available, it's also very good with small frozen peas.

3 oz (80 g) pancetta or pork belly
3 tbsp olive oil
3 tbsp (50 g) butter
1 small yellow onion
1 handful flat-leaf parsley
14 oz (400 g) peas
5 cups (1 liter) beef or other meat stock
10 oz (300 g) Arborio rice
1.7 oz (50 g) Parmesan
salt
black pepper

Finely chop the pancetta/pork belly and fry in the olive oil and half of the butter. Finely chop the onion and sauté until soft, without browning it. Finely chop the parsley and add half of it to the pan.

Add peas, pour in some of the stock, and let simmer for a few minutes. Add the remaining stock and Arborio rice and simmer until the rice is al dente. Stir in the rest of the butter and freshly grated Parmesan. Season with salt and freshly ground black pepper. Top it off with the remaining chopped leaf parsley and serve.

Zuppa di prosciutto e melone
Melon and prosciutto soup, Emilia-Romagna

A fresh, summery, rich, and flavorful soup. The melon you use should be very ripe. Sniff the calyx of the melon; if it smells really sweet, it's ripe. If it is not ripe enough you may add some sugar to really bring out the flavors.

1 cantaloupe, 2–3 lbs (1–1 ½ kg)
sugar (optional)
juice of 1 orange
juice of ¼ lemon
coarse salt
black pepper
4 large slices of prosciutto di Parma

Halve the melon and remove the seeds and the rind. Cut the fruit into smaller pieces. Puree in a mixer or food processor. Add sugar if necessary.

Add freshly squeezed orange juice. Adjust the acidity with freshly squeezed lemon juice. Season with salt. It should taste fresh, a little sweet, but not salty; the salt is really only added to enhance the flavors. Grind pepper on top.

Shred the prosciutto. Stir about one fourth of the ham into the soup and scoop into 4 bowls. Place the remaining prosciutto on top of the soup in each bowl. Top it off with some freshly ground pepper and serve.

Stracciatella
Roman-style egg-drop soup, Lazio

Possibly the simplest soup in the Italian culinary canon. It may not look the best to the rest of the world, but it tastes great. Of course, it's best if you can use home-made stock, but canned stock or broth is also fine. A common dish in Rome and Lazio.

Stracciato means "torn," "cut," or "rags." Some say the dish got this name because it looks like an old rag used for cleaning. The soup has nothing in common with the ice cream except for the name.

4 eggs
4 tbsp durum wheat flour
4 tbsp Parmesan
5 cups (1 liter) veal or chicken stock
salt
black pepper
pinch of grated nutmeg
flat-leaf parsley

Whisk eggs, durum wheat, freshly grated Parmesan, and a ladle-full of stock in a bowl. Season the blend with salt, freshly ground black pepper, and nutmeg.

Bring the stock to a boil in a pot. Remove from stove. Stir the egg mixture into the stock one tablespoon at a time. The egg should look like long threads in the stock.

Return the pot to the stove and simmer, being careful not to let it boil. Season with salt and pepper. Top it off with chopped parsley before serving.

Minestrone
Rich vegetable soup, Tuscany

Literally, *minestrone* means "big soup"—in other words, a soup that is thick and filling. This recipe is adapted for different seasons and according to which vegetables are available locally. The mushrooms used are also different depending on whether you're in the North or the South. Ligurians in the northwest use fewer tomatoes and they add pesto. In Puglia they use lots of tomatoes, eggplant, and various kinds of large bell peppers. In Friuli–Venezia Giulia they add potatoes and barley. In Calabria they add peperoncino for an extra kick. In Piedmont and Lombardy rice is used instead of pasta. All kinds of beans, leafy greens, asparagus, leeks, Savoy cabbage, and other cabbage varieties are great in this soup as well. Always remember to save the Parmesan rind, which is the outer hard part that remains when you've used all of the softer cheese. There is no surface treatment or wax on Parmesan; it's cheese all the way through. The rinds are perfect for adding a rich flavor to soups. Just make sure to fish them out and discard them before serving.

Minestrone is prepared in two different ways. To make *minestrone col soffrito* you begin by browning pancetta or bacon and then sauté the vegetables, each in turn, before finally adding the stock. To make *Minestrone a crudo,* you add the vegetables directly to the stock. Making a *minestrone* should take a lot of time but not much effort; it just needs time to simmer or stew in order for the flavors to develop. It is therefore important to wait until the very end to add seasoning.

Minestrone can be served during the summertime, as it's also good cold. But do not eat it directly out of the fridge. If you do, it won't taste right, so be sure to let it sit out at room temperature for a while.

1.7 oz (50 g) pancetta
olive oil
1 yellow onion
1 carrot
1 celery stalk
½ lb (250 g) potatoes
½ lb (250 g) Swiss chard or spinach
1 lb (450 g) zucchini
3.5 oz (100 g) haricot verts or green beans
3 plum tomatoes or ½ can crushed tomatoes
1 handful fresh basil leaves
crumbled Parmesan
beef broth
salt
black pepper

¾ cup (1 ½ dl) canned cannellini or borlotti beans,
*   or similar dried or soaked*
3.5 oz (100 g) short pasta, such as risoni or stelline
flat-leaf parsley
Parmesan (optional)

Shred or dice the pancetta. Fry it in olive oil in a pot until it releases its fat.

Add finely chopped yellow onion and sauté until soft but do not brown. Dice the carrot and sauté until soft. Add finely chopped celery and sauté until soft as well. Dice the potatoes and sauté with the rest.

Rinse chard or spinach and sauté until the liquids have evaporated. Cut the ends off of the zucchini, dice, and add to the saucepan. Stir in the haricot verts or green beans, snapping the ends off the green beans before adding.

Blanch, peel, seed, and dice the tomatoes and add to the pot. Stir in the basil and crumbled Parmesan. Pour in enough stock to cover the vegetables. Season with salt and freshly ground pepper.

Let simmer for about 2 hours. Check in on the soup now and then. When an hour and a half has elapsed, rinse the canned beans and stir into the soup. Add the pasta towards the end of the cooking time and continue to simmer until the pasta is just al dente. Season with salt and pepper again as needed. Drizzle olive oil on top and serve with chopped parsley and freshly grated Parmesan.

PASTA

Pasta is without a doubt most popular and most common as a *primo*.

Not a day goes by without pasta in Italy.

Many people eat it multiple times a day.

When someone calls up and says *"Butta la pasta!"*—Throw the pasta in the water—it means they'll be home soon.

Fresh pasta or dried pasta: one is not better than the other. They have different functions and distinct tastes. Dried pasta has its own special dishes and the same with fresh pasta, so they're not as interchangeable as one might think.

The creativity that Italians bring to pasta dishes never ceases to impress. Stuffed pasta, oven-baked pasta, and pasta with sauce—but not too much! The pasta is the star, not the sauce.

With hundreds of pasta varieties and a lot of different opinions as to which works best in which dish, there is also fuel for endless discussions.

But one thing is for certain: The sauce waits for the pasta, the pasta never waits for the sauce. *La pasta non aspetta!*

Spaghetti aglio, olio e peperoncino
Spaghetti with garlic, oil, and chili pepper, Abruzzo

This dish has spread throughout Italy but it originated in Chieti in Abruzzo, where it's made with *diavolillo*, the little devil, a super-hot chili pepper. Small dried chili peppers or dried and crushed chili pepper, so-called chili flakes, work just fine.

This is a perfect dish for when you are hungry but can't be bothered to make a huge meal or when you get home late at night and need a quick and filling snack. You can almost always order this in Italy even if it's not on the menu

It can be hard to say exactly how much chili pepper you should use because the potency varies, but it's supposed to be hot, and you shouldn't be skimpy with the olive oil either.

Simple dishes like this one reveal the great difference between different types of pasta. A more expensive spaghetti made with the best durum wheat, rolled through brass nozzles, and dried slowly will have a somewhat rough surface, which will pick up the delicious oil quite well.

3 garlic cloves
½ cup (1 ¼ dl) olive oil
1–3 small dried peperoncino, depending on potency
About 1 lb (500 g) spaghetti
flat-leaf parsley
black pepper

Set the pasta water on the stove.

Crush the garlic cloves and sauté them until soft in olive oil in a frying pan along with the peperoncino. Be careful to avoid burning the garlic; it should take on a golden color, but nothing darker than that. Remove the peperoncino. Boil the spaghetti in salted water until al dente, with a small core of uncooked pasta at the center. Drain the pasta and place in the pan with the oil. Stir well so that all the pasta is covered in olive oil.

Chop the parsley and sprinkle on top; grind black pepper over the dish, toss, and serve.

Spaghetti con piselli, pancetta e menta
Spaghetti with peas, pancetta, and mint, Sicily

14 oz (400 g) Spaghetti
3.5 oz (100 g) pancetta or bacon
2 tbsp olive oil
1 small dried peperoncino
3 garlic cloves
7 oz (200 g) frozen peas
1 handful of fresh mint leaves
black pepper
approximately ½ cup (1 dl) grated pecorino, Parmesan, or bread crumbs

Boil the spaghetti in abundant salted water.

Shred or finely chop the pancetta. Fry in olive oil so that it releases the fat but not so much that it turns crispy. Add the peperoncino.

Peel the garlic cloves and let them brown in the olive oil. Remove the garlic and the peperoncino. Add the peas and heat them in the pan. Stir in the pasta and chopped mint. Grind black pepper on top.

Serve with pecorino, Parmesan, or bread crumbs browned golden in some olive oil, which is the poor man's substitute for Parmesan.

Spaghetti alla puttanesca

Spaghetti with olives, capers, and anchovies, Campania

An "emergency" pasta made with ingredients you can usually find stocked in your pantry. The name means "spaghetti of the prostitutes," as does its other name, *spaghetti alla buonadonna*. It is said to date back to the 1950s when state brothels—called closed houses, *case chiuse*, because the windows were always closed and covered to keep people from looking in—were still up and running in Italy. The prostitutes only went food shopping once a week, most likely because there was a taboo about their being seen in public. The result of this was foods prepared with preserves, like this dish. It just goes to show that the most popular dishes usually come with an anecdote.

about 1 lb (500 g) spaghetti
3 garlic cloves
3 anchovy filets
14 oz (400 g) pureed or whole preserved tomatoes
1–2 small dried chili pepper, crushed
2 tbsp olive oil
4 oz (120 g) pitted olives
4 tbsp capers
parsley

Boil the spaghetti in abundant salted water.

Chop the garlic. Rinse and chop the anchovies. If you are using whole preserved tomatoes, chop these as well. Save the tomato broth and set aside.

Sauté the garlic, anchovies, and hot pepper in olive oil in a saucepan without browning the garlic but allowing the anchovies to soften. Chop the olives and add to the saucepan with capers and pureed or chopped tomatoes. Let everything simmer for 5 minutes.

Drain the pasta when it is al dente. Mix the spaghetti and sauce in a large bow or directly in the saucepan. Sprinkle chopped parsley on top and serve.

Pasta alla carbonara
Carbonara as it's made in Trastevere, Lazio

Spaghetti alla carbonara is a Roman classic. In Rome it is commonly served the way we ate it in Trastevere, with rigatoni. Ideally, it should be made with *guanciale*, salted and air-dried pork jowl, but pancetta is also common. If none of these are available, bacon will have to do. The cheese should be *pecorino romano*, not parmesan, and cream and parsley should be omitted.

14 oz (400 g) rigatoni or spaghetti
About ¾ cup (1 ½ dl) freshly grated Pecorino romano
3.5 oz (100 g) guanciale, pancetta, or bacon
Olive oil
1 garlic clove (optional)
2 large eggs
Freshly ground black pepper

Heat water for pasta, then add the rigatoni or spaghetti when the water has reached a boil. You'll have time to finish everything else while this is cooking.

Dice the guanciale and sauté in a large saucepan with some olive oil. If you wish to include garlic, crush the garlic clove with the knife blade so that the skin cracks open, or use it with the skin (this is called *aglio in camicia*, or garlic wearing a shirt). Let the garlic sauté with the meat but remove it before it gains any color.

Lightly whisk the eggs in a bowl with half of the pecorino.

Remove the pasta from the stove before it is completely done—it will cook a little bit in the pan as well. Drain the pasta in a strainer but save some of the hot

water. Add the pasta to the saucepan and mix with the guanciale. Remove the saucepan from the stove and quickly pour the egg mixture in the pan and stir. Add some hot water and blend if you wish. Grind black pepper on top and serve with the remaining cheese.

The pan is not to be placed back on the stove once the eggs are added. The carbonara should be creamy. If it is too hot, you will end up with an egg casserole instead.

Pasta ai zucchini e pomodori freschi
Pasta with zucchini and fresh tomatoes

A typical summer dish. Buy vegetables fresh from the harvest and prepare them in the simplest way possible. Quick and delicious!

1 small yellow onion
Olive oil
2 garlic cloves
1 lb 5 oz (600 g) zucchini
10 oz (300 g) tomatoes
Fresh basil (optional)
¼ cup (½ dl) dry white wine (optional)
14 oz (400 g) pasta
Salt
Freshly ground black pepper
Parsley (optional)

Finely chop the onion and sauté in olive oil until it becomes translucent, taking care not to brown it. Crush the garlic with the knife blade or mince it. Add to the pan and let it sauté without browning.

Dice or slice the zucchini. Heat some olive oil in a separate pan. Brown the zucchini on high heat. Add to the other pan with the onion and garlic.

Dice the tomatoes, taking care to remove the seeds. Sauté briefly with the other ingredients. The tomatoes should not fall apart but rather should maintain some firmness. If you wish, you might add some shredded basil leaves and white wine near the end of the cooking time.

Boil the pasta until it is almost fully cooked, then strain. Add to the pan and toss with the sauce and zucchini. Season with salt and pepper. You may add basil and chopped parsley for garnish.

How to boil pasta the right way

Short, thick dried pasta is usually served with rich meat sauces, whereas long, thin dried pasta is served with thinner, lighter sauces, like those made with shellfish and fish.

If the pasta is served as *primo* in a full meal (complete with *antipasto*, *primo*, *secondo*, and *dolci*), allow about 1.7 ounces (50 grams) of pasta for each person. If the pasta is part of a lighter meal allow 2.4–2.8 ounces (70–80 grams) per person. If serving the pasta as a meal on its own allow about 3.5 oz (100 g) per person.

Boil the pasta in a generous amount of water, 4 cups (1 liter) per 3.5 oz (100 g) of pasta.

When the water is boiling, add 1 ½ tsp salt per 4 cups (1 liter) of water (doubled, this works out to 1 tbsp/8 cups [2 liters]). It should taste like saltwater, and the pasta cooked in it should be flavorful enough that you could eat it as is.

Do not add oil to the water. The oil will stick to the pasta, which is where you want the sauce and other flavors to stick instead.

When you boil lasagna you can add olive oil so that the pieces do not stick to each other.

Pour all of the pasta into the water at the same time. Stir right away. Long pasta takes a while to soften so that it can be properly submerged in the water, but stir as soon as you can. To bring the water to a boil again as soon as possible after adding the pasta you can cover the pot with a lid, but be sure to remove the lid as soon as it starts boiling; if you don't, it will boil over. Continue to boil uncovered.

Do not boil the pasta for the amount of time stated on the package. That way you run the risk of overcooking it, so taste the pasta a few minutes before the recommended time has elapsed. Remove the pasta when it is al dente, in other words when it is not quite done. Recipes will sometimes have you cook the pasta with the sauce for a bit, in which case, you'll have to shorten the boiling time.

If possible, boil the pasta in a pot made specifically for pasta and equipped with a colander. This way you can easily save the pasta water for use in the sauce if desired. Fresh pasta needs even more water for boiling than dried, because it absorbs more water. If you boil in a regular large pot remember to save a little bit of the boiling water when you're draining the pasta.

One good trick is to place the colander in a serving bowl and let the water drain into the bowl (you will remove the colander later). This way you both warm the serving bowl and you save the water.

You do not have to be very meticulous when you pour the pasta into the colander as much of the remaining water will evaporate and the pasta will also absorb a lot of it.

Do not cool the pasta in cold water. If you do, you'll rinse away much of the starch. The only time you should cool pasta in cold water is when making a pasta salad.

Mix the drained pasta with some of the sauce right away so that the pasta doesn't stick together, or mix with all of the sauce if the recipe calls for it.

The pasta never waits for the sauce. The sauce should wait for the pasta.

The pasta is the star of the dish and should never be served with too much sauce. It should be pasta with sauce, *not* sauce with pasta.

Sometimes you might want to serve the pasta directly from the pan in order to hang on to as much of the sauce as possible, as you would with a simple *aglio, olio, e peperoncino*. In that case you'll need a large pan. This is often also when you'll need to use some of the boiling water.

Because pasta cools quickly, it should be served on warm plates.

If you're using olive oil in the sauce, it may be a good idea to drizzle some fresh (unheated) olive oil—*olio crudo*—over the pasta right before serving.

> *The pasta never waits for the sauce.*
> *The sauce waits for the pasta.*

Pasta alla Norma
Pasta with fried eggplant, Sicily

The Teatro Massimo Bellini, a famous opera house in Catania, on the eastern coast of Sicily, is named after opera composer Vincenzo Bellini, a native of the city. It is said that this dish acquired its name after the inauguration of the theater on May 31 in 1890 with a performance of Bellini's *Norma*. By naming this pasta after Bellini's masterwork, the proud inhabitants of Catania honored the composer by associating him with a truly classic local dish.

In Italy, every beloved food seems to have some kind of a myth surrounding its origins. Or multiple. Another myth says that this dish got its name in the 1920s when a well-known actor of the day told the chef that his pasta was "as good as *Norma*."

In Sicily, the dish is served with *ricotta salata*, which is a salted, pressed, and aged sheep's milk ricotta.

The pasta used is either penne or spaghetti.

The Bellini, a cocktail made with prosecco and peach puree, is not named after the composer but rather after the fifteenth-century painter Giovanni Bellini. The color of the drink reminded Giuseppe Cipriani—the owner of Harry's bar in Venice and the creator of the drink—of the color of the cloth worn by a saint in one of Bellini's paintings. Or so the legend goes . . .

1 large eggplant
salt
1 yellow onion or 2 garlic cloves
olive oil
1 small dried peperoncino, crushed (optional)
2 cups (5 dl) strained tomatoes
black pepper
14 oz (400 g) penne or spaghetti
3.5 oz (100 g) grated ricotta salata or pecorino
fresh basil

Thinly slice the eggplant or cut it into short batonnets as shown above. Salt generously and let it drain for at least an hour under the weight of several dishes (or anything else you may have around the kitchen that is fairly heavy and has a flat surface). Rinse off the salt and dry. As an alternative, you can heat the eggplant on high in the microwave for a couple of minutes until warm, then dry. The original reason behind this process was to remove the bitter taste of the eggplant. Today's eggplants are less bitter, but you still need to drain and dry them in order to prevent them from absorbing too much oil during cooking.

Finely chop the onion or, if using garlic, crush the cloves gently with the flat side of a knife. Heat some olive oil to a saucepan and sauté onions until soft, without browning. If using peperoncino, add it to the pan and sauté it with the garlic.

Add the strained tomatoes and let them cook down to a third of the volume. Season the sauce with freshly ground black pepper.

Heat olive oil in a frying pan and brown the eggplant.

Boil the pasta, then drain.

Mix the pasta with half of the ricotta salata. Stir in the tomato sauce and basil leaves. Season with black pepper and stir well.

Distribute the pasta into plates and arrange the eggplant on top. Top it off with more ricotta and garnish with basil leaves.

Pasta al forno di Sophia Loren
Sophia Loren's baked pasta, Campania

According to legendary Neapolitan actress Sophia Loren, this is a great dish for entertaining guests. In her 1998 cookbook, Recipes and Memories, she writes that *pasta al forno* is the perfect dish to bring to a party because you can easily prepare it in advance and finish baking it when you get there. You can also bring it as a present, or as a ready-to-eat to a picnic.

This is *pasta al forno* the Neapolitan way. Here we use a blend of different ground meats, but ground pork or veal works just fine. Furthermore, you can stir in a little bit of whatever meat you have lying around: salami, prosciutto di Parma, boiled ham, bacon, smoked pork belly, or pancetta.

Meat sauce:
1 yellow onion
olive oil
1 celery stalk
1 carrot
1.3 lbs (600 g) mixed ground meat (beef, pork, veal, etc.)
½ cup (1 dl) red wine
about 1 lb (500 g) strained tomatoes
6 basil leaves
salt
black pepper

about 1 lb (500 g) penne or similar short pasta

1 batch béchamel

1 ¼ cup (2 ½ dl) (about 2 oz [65 g]) freshly grated Parmesan

Finely chop the onion and sauté in a few tablespoons of olive oil until it becomes soft and translucent. Finely chop the celery and add to the pan. Finely chop the carrot and sauté. Stir in the meat and brown.

Add the wine and bring the mixture to a boil. Add the strained tomatoes and basil leaves and simmer for about half an hour, stirring occasionally. The sauce should not be runny, but be sure to add water if it is too thick. Season with salt and freshly ground black pepper.

Prepare the béchamel according to the recipe on the right.

Preheat the oven to 400 F (200 C). Boil the pasta in generously salted water and strain when almost fully cooked, then blend with half of the meat sauce. Spread out a third of this in a baking dish. Cover with a third of

the remaining meat sauce. Use a third of the béchamel and cheese to create the next layer. Repeat for two more layers. Finish with the béchamel and Parmesan. Bake for 20 minutes until nicely browned.

Up until this final step, you can keep the covered baking dish in the fridge. Cover with foil and bake for 20–30 minutes, then remove the foil and bake until the top layer is golden brown.

Besciamella
Italian béchamel

Italian béchamel is a lot thicker than the French version. *Besciamella* has the texture of vanilla cream and isn't as runny as the French sauce. Of course, the Italians claim that it originated in Italy. This is the sauce used in lasagna and other baked pasta dishes.

2 ½ cups (6 dl) milk
3 tbsp (50 g) butter
⅓ cup (40 g) flour
salt
black pepper
nutmeg

Heat the milk in a saucepan. In a separate saucepan, melt the butter. Use a saucepan with a thick bottom; it will distribute the heat more evenly so that the sauce doesn't burn. Whisk in the flour so that it blends evenly with the butter. Whisk in the milk a little at a time until the butter and flour blend has dissolved.

Bring the mixture to a boil then reduce the heat and let it simmer for about 5 minutes. Stir constantly so that the sauce doesn't burn; burnt béchamel is not pleasant tasting. Season with salt, black pepper, and freshly grated nutmeg.

Pietro Fioriniello

AS A CHILD PIETRO PLAYED SOCCER among fennel, eggplant, and zucchini plants outside of Naples. Since then, food has always been the center of his attention.

"I grew up immersed in the delicious smell of tomato sauce. As soon as my mother left the stove I was there to make my mark on whatever was cooking. I stayed at home and experimented with different flavors."

Pietro's father's specialty was *pasta e fagioli*. When Pietro was little, his father worked nights and made tomato sauce at the Cirio preserve factory. When he came home at 6 in the morning he sometimes brought a *pizza fritta*, a large fried pizza with ricotta, a variety of pancetta, and black pepper.

"That was breakfast. It smelled wonderful! It was like a party."

Later in life, Pietro left his technical high school and enrolled in a cooking and hospitality school in Sorrento.

"It was financed by the regional government. There were a lot of students—but the heads of the school took all the money. A classic Neapolitan business. I was 16 years old."

Pietro made a living by preparing fish, shellfish, and other food at the beach in Positano. And when he and his friends traveled around Italy, he would do the cooking.

"One summer in Florence I met a Swedish girl at the Piazzale Michelangelo. I hadn't even turned eighteen. And so I ended up in Sweden. And it was there that I attended cooking school. When I arrived I was shocked. I had never seen people eat so poorly. A lot has changed since then. Nowadays, people eat well in Sweden."

PIETRO TAKES HIS INSPIRATION FOR COOKING from all over Italy. This kind of mentality may be possible in Naples today, but it wasn't that way when he was young.

"My mother and father still eat very traditionally. They will maybe eat pesto, but aside from that they only eat Neapolitan dishes. But things are changing in Naples. Today you can even find kebab at the central station."

Pietro Fioriniello runs La Cucina Italiana in Gothenburg and has been awarded the Bib Gourmand in the Michelin Guide. The Italian chamber of commerce has awarded him a *marchio di qualità* for his commitment to spreading Italian food culture.

Pasta e fagioli
Pasta with beans, Campania

Variations on this dish are made all over the country. In the north, pasta e fagioli is more like a soup, whereas Naples's *pasta fazul*, as it is called in the local dialect, is quite dry (although Neapolitans will still eat it with a spoon).

Cannellini beans are common in the south and borlotti are more common in the north. In Naples, they use various types of pastas in this dish, often a mix of different leftover pastas.

2 oz (60 g) pancetta
3 tbsp olive oil
½ yellow onion
3 garlic cloves
1 stalk leaf celery
about 10 oz (300 g) dried
    cannellini or borlotti bean
    (let soak in water for
    24 hours before cooking)
about 10 oz (300 g) pasta
1 twig rosemary
2–3 tbsp tomato sauce,
canned diced tomatoes, or
tomato puree
salt
black pepper

Heat 1 tbsp olive oil in a saucepan. Dice the pancetta and sauté half of it in the oil. Finely chop the yellow onion and sauté with the pancetta until soft, but do not brown. Mince the garlic and sauté without browning. Finely chop celery and add half of it to the saucepan with the other ingredients.

Place the beans in the saucepan and add cold water to 1–2 inches above the beans. Stir occasionally, adding extra water as needed.

Add the pasta and two garlic cloves *in camicia* (unpeeled) to the saucepan along with some finely chopped rosemary. Bring to a boil, stirring continuously. Add more water to the saucepan if needed. The contents should cook down until you have a creamy blend of beans and pasta.

Add the tomato sauce, canned diced tomatoes, or tomato puree and continue to cook.

Fold in the rest of the pancetta and celery along with 2 tbsp olive oil. Season with salt and freshly ground pepper. Garnish with celery leaves..

Orechiette ai broccoli
Orecchiette with broccoli, Puglia

1.3 lbs (600 g) broccoli
about 1 lb (500 g) orecchiette
3 garlic cloves
1 fresh red chili or 1–2 dried peperoncini, depending on
*   strength*
4 tbsp olive oil
salt
black pepper

Cut the broccoli into small florets, cutting away the stalks if they are tough. Cut the stalks into smaller pieces. Boil in salted water for a couple of minutes. Strain, saving the water the broccoli was boiled in. Cool the broccoli in cold water.

Pour the water you used to boil the broccoli into a pot, add some additional water, add salt, and bring to a boil. Use this water to cook the pasta.

Heat some olive oil in a pan and sauté the garlic, minced, along with the peperoncino. Add the broccoli as well.

Strain the pasta, saving some of the water. Add the pasta and broccoli to the pan with the oil, garlic, and peperoncino and stir, adding some of the water the pasta was boiled in if necessary.

Spaghetti cacio e pepe
Spaghetti with cheese and black pepper, Lazio

A much-loved pasta dish, especially in Rome. It is rarely listed on the menu, but you can always order it.

about 1 lb (500 g) spaghetti
3.5 oz (100 g) pecorino Romano
black pepper
flat-leaf parsley (optional)

Boil the pasta in a generous amount of salted water. Cook until almost ready; there should still be a small hard core in the center of the noodle when you strain it. Save some of the water.

Stir freshly grated pecorino Romano into the pasta and season with freshly ground pepper. Add a couple of table-spoons of the water the pasta was boiled in and stir. Garnish with some chopped parsley if desired. Serve right away.

Cappellini al forno con prosciutto e mozzarella
Baked capellini with prosciutto and mozzarella

A delicious casserole showcasing a thin pasta. Cappel-lini, also known as angel hair, is the thinnest spaghetti available, but vermicelli also works well. This dish can also be made with leftover pasta.

bread crumbs
about 1 lb (500 g) cappellini
3.5 oz (100 g) Parmesan
7 tbsp (100 g) butter, plus extra for greasing baking dish
black pepper
3 eggs
5 oz (150 g) prosciutto di Parma, sliced
8–9 oz (250 g) mozzarella

Preheat the oven to 480 F (250 C). Butter a baking dish and sprinkle with bread crumbs.

Boil the pasta in a generous amount of salted water until it is almost ready. Grate the Parmesan. Strain the pasta, return it to the pot, and add ¾ of the Parmesan and ¾ of the butter. Season with freshly ground pepper and stir.

Spread out half of the pasta in a baking dish. Whisk the eggs and pour half of the mixture on top. Shred the prosciutto slices. Dice the Mozzarella. Cover the pasta with a layer of prosciutto and mozzarella.

Cover this with the rest of the pasta and pour the rest of the eggs on top. Sprinkle with bread crumbs and the remaining Parmesan. Top it off with scoops of the remaining butter. Bake until golden brown and serve right away.

Pesto genovese
Genovese pesto, Liguria

There are many recipes for pesto and even more arguments as to why one is right and the others are wrong. But the ingredients are always basically the same: pine nuts, Parmesan, pecorino, garlic, olive oil, and sweet-smelling basil. Different preparations simply call for more or less of a given ingredient.

Because this is a Ligurian specialty, the olive oil used should be mild, not a peppery one like those hailing from Tuscany or Sicily. Pesto should not be heated. In Liguria pesto is often served with long beans (green beans or haricot verts), sliced boiled potatoes, and trofie, a small, screw-like pasta.

1 oz (30 g) pine nuts
1.7 oz (50 g) fresh basil leaves
1 garlic clove
4 tbsp freshly grated Parmesan
2 tbsp freshly grated pecorino
½–⅓ cup (1–1¼ dl) olive oil
salt
14 oz (400 g) pasta

Dry-toast the pine nuts quickly in a hot frying pan to enhance the flavors, making sure not to burn them. Let cool.

A real pesto should be prepared using a mortar and pestle, but a food processor works just as well. Place the pine nuts, basil, and peeled and crushed garlic in the food processor and chop. Add Parmesan and pecorino and pour in the oil in a thin stream while the food processor is working until the pesto has a nice texture. Boil and strain the pasta, stir in the pesto, and serve.

Tagliatelle con salsa di noci
Tagliatelle with walnut pesto, Liguria

Walnuts are a big part of Italian cuisine. They grow all over the country, but you find the best ones in Liguria and Campania. This is like Ligurian pesto but it is made with walnuts. In Campania, they often add peperoncino along with the walnuts.

10.5 oz (200 g) walnuts
1 handful flat-leaf parsley
1 garlic clove
1 cup (2 dl) olive oil
1 oz (30 g) Parmesan
½ cup (1 dl) whipping cream
salt
14 oz (400 g) tagliatelle

Dry-toast the walnuts in a hot skillet until they release their aroma and start to color. Let cool.

Place walnuts, parsley, and peeled and crushed garlic in a food processor and finely chop. Add the olive oil in a thin stream while the food processor is working. Stir in the freshly grated Parmesan and cream. Season with salt.

If using a mortar and pestle: finely chop the ingredients, add to the mortar and grind, stir in the oil, and mix.

Boil and strain the pasta, mix in the pesto, and serve.

Farfalle con pesto di rughetta
Farfalle with arugula pesto, Puglia

Rucola, *ruchetta, rughetta, ruca, erba ruga, gruritta, aruca*—
there are many regional words for this peppery and
delicious leafy green. Wild arugula is known as rucola
selvatica in Italy. It is especially common in southern
Italy to gather and prepare wild herbs and greens—even
if they're growing in a ditch on the side of the road.

On Ischia, an island in the Bay of Naples, they make
an amaro—a bitter digestive liqueur—out of arugula,
known as rucolino.

6–7 oz (180–200 g) arugula
1 small handful flat-leaf parsley
1 oz (30 g) walnuts
1 garlic clove
1.5 oz (40 g) pecorino
⅔ cup (¾ dl) olive oil
salt
black pepper
1.7 oz (50 g) farfalle
14 oz (400 g) fresh cherry tomatoes

Place arugula, parsley, walnuts, and peeled and crushed
garlic in a food processor. Chop thoroughly. Grate almost
all of the pecorino and add to the arugula mixture.

Add olive oil in a thin stream while the machine is working.
Mix until smooth. Season with salt and fresh ground pepper.

Boil the pasta in a generous amount of salted water, then
strain, saving some of the water. Mix pasta and pesto
together in a bowl. Add the pasta water if needed.

Halve or quarter the tomatoes and add to the pasta.
Shave the remaining pecorino on top and serve.

Wild arugula growing just
outside of Trapani, Sicily.

Spaghetti alle vongole
Spaghetti with clams, Campania

Vongole are a kind of clam in the Bay of Naples. You can find them preserved in glass jars and they taste surprisingly good. *Vongole veraci* are considered the best kind.

You can buy other kinds of fresh clams or order them from a fishmonger. Clams are served all along the southern Italian coast and they are also very popular in Rome, where just about every trattoria seems to serve *vongole*. There are two varieties: with tomatoes and without.

2 lbs (1 kg) clams
1–2 garlic wedges
1–2 small peperoncini, depending on strength
4 tbsp olive oil
½ cup (1 dl) dry white wine
14 oz (400 g) spaghetti (or linguine or vermicelli)
flat-leaf parsley
salt
black pepper

Put the pasta water on the stove to boil. Scrub the clams. Discard any that have broken shells or do not close when you knock on them.

Place the clams in a large pot and heat, covered, until they open. Discard any that do not open. Strain the liquid in the pot and set aside.

Crush and peel the garlic and sauté with peperoncino and olive oil in a frying pan. Remove the garlic and *peperoncino* when the garlic starts to gain some color. Place the clams in the pan and stir. Add the wine and the stock and let simmer for a couple of minutes.

Boil the pasta; ideally, it should be ready by the time the clam sauce has finished simmering. Pour the pasta on top and mix with the clam sauce in the pan. Sprinkle chopped parsley on top. Season with salt and black pepper, mix, and serve right away.

With tomatoes:

about 1 lb (500 g) ripe tomatoes

Blanch, peel, seed, and dice the tomatoes. Prepare the dish according to the recipe above, but add the tomatoes when you remove the garlic and peperoncino from the pan. Continue as above. The tomatoes should not be cooked until soft, but rather should be almost raw.

Tagliolini agli scampi
Tagliolini with langoustines

This dish is traditionally prepared with langoustines, called scampi and scamponi, the first smaller and the latter larger, but it can also be made with raw shrimp, which are easier to find in the US. Tagliolini is a long pasta that looks like spaghetti. No Parmesan or pecorino with this recipe.

14 oz (400 g) fresh uncooked langoustines or large uncooked shrimp
1 small yellow onion
1 celery stalk
1 carrot
3 tbsp olive oil
flat-leaf parsley
1 tsp tomato puree
about 10 oz (275 g) fresh tagliolini

Peel and devein the langoustines or shrimp and set aside. Save the shells.

Chop onion, celery, and carrot. Place the langoustine or shrimp shells, onion, celery, and carrot in a pot. Cover with water, bring to a boil, and let simmer for 15 minutes. Strain the vegetables and shells and save the stock.

Heat olive oil in a pan. Sauté the langoustines or shrimp for a couple of minutes. Sprinkle chopped parsley on top. Mix tomato puree with some of the homemade stock in a bowl then add to the pan.

Boil the pasta in salted water and strain. Empty into the pan with the sauce and mix well. Serve right away.

Paglia e fieno
Pasta with mushrooms, prosciutto di Parma, and cream, Tuscany

Green and white tagliatelle or fettuccine is called *paglia e fieno*, "straw and hay." Feel free to use fresh pasta. Use a mix of mushrooms you have at home or that you can find at the store, like champignons, brown champignons, portabellas, porcini, chanterelles, oyster mushrooms, and pioppini. You can also make a variation by using a quality boiled ham instead of prosciutto di Parma.

14 oz (400 g) green and white tagliatelle or fettuccine
about 10 oz (300 g) fresh mushrooms
juice of ½ lemon
1 small shallot
1 garlic clove
3 tbsp butter
salt
black pepper
5 oz (150 g) prosciutto di Parma
½ handful flat-leaf parsley
½ cup (1 dl) whipping cream
3 tbsp butter
½ cup (1 dl) whipping cream
1.7 oz (50 g) freshly grated Parmesan plus extra for serving
fresh basil

Rinse and dry the mushrooms and cut into thin slices. Place in a bowl and add 1 tbsp of lemon juice. Mix. Finely chop the shallot and garlic. Melt 3 tablespoons butter in a pan. Sauté the shallot until soft, but without browning it. Add the garlic and continue to sauté, but do not brown. Put the heat on high, add the mushrooms, stir, and sauté until all of the butter has been absorbed. Lower the heat slightly. Season with salt

and black pepper. When the mushrooms have released their water, increase the heat once more and cook off the water, stirring constantly. Reduce heat to medium.

Shred the prosciutto di Parma or ham and add to the pan. Sauté, stirring constantly. Finely chop the parsley and add. Continue to sauté and stir. Add ½ cup (1 dl) heavy cream and let it simmer until it thickens. Season with some salt and pepper and remove from the stove.

Heat a large frying pan. Melt 3 tbsp butter, add ½ cup (1 dl) heavy cream, and bring to a boil until the mixture is well blended. Turn the heat off and add some of the lemon juice.

Boil the pasta until it is almost ready and strain. Add to the pan with the butter and cream. Mix over low heat until the pasta is coated with the cream. Add half of the mushroom sauce and continue to mix. Add Parmesan and stir well. Remove from the stove. Distribute the remaining mushroom sauce and basil leaves on top of the pasta. Serve right away, with extra Parmesan if desired.

Ragù alla carne macinata
Ground meat sauce, Naples, Campania

Dare to be simple. You might not even need salt and black pepper for this sauce. Taste the finished product before seasoning; you'll find that it tastes great just as it is. How many basil leaves you need will depend on how large they are and how they taste.

2 garlic cloves
4 tbsp olive oil
10.5 oz (300 g) ground veal or mixed ground meat
¾ cup (1 ½ dl) dry white wine
14–17 oz (400–500 g) strained tomatoes
fresh basil
14 oz (400 g) short pasta, such as paccheri, penne, or rigatoni
pecorino or Parmesan
flat-leaf parsley

Sauté the garlic—either whole with the peel or crushed without the peel—in olive oil in a saucepan over medium heat until it starts to brown. Add the meat and brown. Add the wine and bring to a boil. Add the tomatoes and some basil leaves and let simmer for at least 1 hour, stirring occasionally. Add more basil leaves and/or water as needed. The sauce should thicken and darken.

Boil the pasta in salted water until almost fully cooked. Strain and mix with the sauce in the saucepan. Let it cook together for 1 minute. Serve with freshly grated pecorino or Parmesan and chopped flat-leaf parsley.

Ragù alla Bolognese
Ground meat sauce from Bologna, Emilia–Romagna

During the 1970s the house of commerce in Bologna and *l'Accademia Italiana della Cucina di Bologna* decided to collect all existing recipes for this sauce. On October 17, 1982 the house of commerce presented the official one. But what difference did that make? Every family still claims that the recipe they use is the original.

Bologna's meat sauce is lighter and milder than the Neapolitan version. The tomatoes don't dominate the sauce and the milk rounds out all of the flavors. It is not at all as fluid as the Bolognese sauce one sometimes encounters abroad; to the contrary, it's quite dry. And, as always, the pasta should be the star, meaning that there should be more pasta than sauce. Some use chicken liver; some say that there should only be pancetta (the unsmoked kind, although in emergencies you can use bacon); and others say that red wine should be used instead of white.

The following recipe is very good and can serve as a starting point. *Ragù* is served with tagliatelle, penne, or another short pasta, but *not* spaghetti.

1 yellow onion
2 celery stalks
2 carrots
olive oil
3.5 oz (100 g) pancetta or prosciutto di Parma
14 oz (400 g) ground meat (pork, veal, or mixed)
½–¾ cup (1 ½ dl) dry white wine
2–3 tbsp tomato puree
¼–½ cup (½–1 dl) milk
salt
black pepper
Parmesan
flat-leaf parsley

Finely chop the onion, celery, and carrots for a *soffrito* (see page 17). You should use about the same amount of each.

Heat some olive oil in a large saucepan. Sauté the onion until soft, stirring to make sure that it does not brown. Add the celery and do the same. When the celery is soft, add the carrots and sauté those as well.

Finely chop pancetta or prosciutto di Parma and sauté, stirring, until it releases its fat. Add the ground meat and brown it, continuing to stir. Add the wine and bring to a boil. Add the tomato puree and stir. Let simmer, covered, for about 1 hour. Add the milk a little at a time as the sauce continues to simmer. Stir occasionally.

Season with salt and freshly ground pepper. Serve with fresh grated Parmesan and chopped flat-leaf parsley.

Pasta al tonno e borecole
Pasta with tuna and bread crumbs, Sicily

Borecole, bread crumbs, are a much-overlooked ingredient. That everything should be saved and nothing wasted was a given in poorer times. Bread crumbs came to be known as the poor man's cheese. Today, bread crumbs are used because they are delicious in their own right.

3 tbsp olive oil
½ cup (1 dl) bread crumbs
1 small yellow onion
4 tbsp olive oil
2 garlic cloves
1–2 small dried peperoncini, depending on strength
4 tbsp dry white wine
1 tin tuna in oil
flat-leaf parsley
about 1 lb (500 g) spaghetti or linguine

Heat olive oil in a pan. Brown the bread crumbs while stirring. Empty onto a plate.

Finely chop the yellow onion. Heat some in olive oil in a large skillet and sauté the onion until soft. Mince the garlic. Let the garlic and peperoncini sauté with the onion until the garlic is soft and just starting to brown. Remove the peperoncini. Add the wine and bring to a boil.

Drain the tuna and chop. Chop the parsley as well. Add tuna and parsley to the pan, stirring carefully, then remove from the stove.

Boil the pasta until it is almost fully cooked in salted water. Strain in a colander, saving some of the pasta water. Mix the pasta in with the ingredients in the pan. Add some of the pasta water if needed. Sprinkle the fried bread crumbs on top and serve.

Fettuccine al filetto di pomodoro
Fettucine with fresh tomato

3.5 oz (100 g) plum tomatoes
4 tbsp butter
1 small yellow onion or 1 shallot
a few basil leaves
salt
3 tbsp dry white wine
about 1 lb (500 g) fresh fettuccine or other fresh pasta

Salt the water you will be cooking the pasta in and bring to a boil. Blanch, peel, seed, and either fillet or dice the tomatoes. As an alternative you can quarter the tomatoes, remove the seeds, and press the skin against the countertop and cut the skin away with a knife.

Melt 3 tbsp of butter in a skillet. Finely chop the onion and sauté until soft but without browning. Add the tomatoes and basil. Salt lightly. Sauté for 1 minute. Add the wine and bring to a boil.

Boil the pasta until it is almost fully cooked and strain. Save some of the pasta water. Add the pasta to the pan along with 1 tbsp butter. Mix the pasta with the tomatoes, basil, and onion. Add some of the pasta water if needed. Serve.

Pasta alla checca
Pasta with fresh tomatoes and mozzarella, Lazio

3–4 firm plum tomatoes
2 portions of mozzarella (½ lb [250 g])
2 handfuls basil leaves
1–2 garlic cloves
4 tbsp olive oil
salt
about 1 lb (500 g) short pasta such as farfalle or mezzi rigatoni
black pepper

Cut, seed, and dice the tomatoes. Dice the mozzarella. Place tomatoes and mozzarella in a bowl. Shred basil leaves and add. Crush and peel garlic and add this to the bowl as well. Add olive oil, salt lightly, and stir. Feel free to let this mixture sit at room temperature for a couple of hours.

Boil the pasta until al dente in salted water, then strain. Remove the garlic from the bowl and discard. Mix the pasta in with the contents of the bowl, grind some black pepper on top, and serve.

Pasta alla norcina
Pasta with sausage and cream, Umbria

Norcia is situated in southeast Umbria and has a 2,500-year history. The city is known for its cured meats, sausages, and hams made from pork and wild boar. In fact, they are so well known for this that *norcineria* is the Italian word for a cured meats store specializing in pork. *Salsiccia*, Italian sausage, is a quick and easy food to prepare. It's good grilled, sautéed, and as a base for pasta sauces. Also, you get all the spices you need for free, because the sausage is already flavored with wine, fennel, and herbs.

Luckily it is starting to become more common in Italian specialty shops abroad as well as at larger supermarkets.

1 small yellow onion
olive oil
7 oz (200 g) salsiccia
½ cup (1 dl) dry white wine
1 cup (2 ½ dl) heavy whipping cream
about 1 lb (500 g) short pasta with holes, for instance rigatoni, conchiglie or lumaconi
1.7 oz (50 g) Parmesan
black pepper

Cut the onion in half and slice it thinly. Sauté in olive oil in a covered saucepan over low heat until the onion is soft and translucent. Do not let it brown.

Remove the skin from the sausage. If you find it difficult to remove the meat from the skin, use a spoon and pull the skin off. Break the meat up with your hands or chop.

Place the meat in the saucepan and sauté. When it has some color, add the wine and let it simmer for a few minutes, then add the cream and continue to simmer, stirring until thick. Grate the Parmesan. Strain the pasta and place in a warm serving bowl. Add the cheese and mix. When the Parmesan has stuck to the pasta, stir in the sauce. Grind black pepper on top, mix, and serve right away.

Tagliatelle al ragù di salsiccia
Tagliatelle with sausage, Emilia–Romagna

1 small yellow onion
1 celery stalk
1 carrot
olive oil
about 1 lb (500 g) salsiccia
½–¾ cup (1 ½ dl) dry white wine
3 oz (80 grams) strained, whole or crushed tomatoes
salt
black pepper
14 oz (400 g) tagliatelle
pecorino or Parmesan
pancetta, bacon, or pork belly (optional)

Finely chop the onion. Finely dice celery and carrot. Heat some olive oil in a pan. If using pancetta, bacon, or pork belly, add to the pan and sauté. Sauté the onion until soft, without browning. Add the celery and sauté for a couple of minutes. Add the carrot and sauté for a couple of minutes more.

Remove the skin from the sausage and break up the meat into bite-sized pieces.

Sauté the sausage meat. Add the wine and let simmer. Add the tomatoes and continue to simmer for 20–30 minutes, stirring occasionally. Season with salt and freshly ground black pepper.

Boil the pasta and strain. Mix with the sauce in a warm serving bowl. Serve with freshly grated pecorino or Parmesan.

Penne all'arrabbiata
Penne with spicy tomato sauce, Lazio

This dish used to be served with spaghetti, but nowadays it is mostly served with penne. Yet the big question is whether the penne should be *penne lisce* (smooth) or *penne rigate* (ridged). Most Romans prefer *penne lisce*, and so do we.

½ fresh red chili or 1–2 small dried peperoncini, depending on
  strength
2 garlic cloves
6 tbsp olive oil
14 oz (400 g) strained or drained crushed tomatoes
1 lb (450 g) penne lisce (smooth)
flat-leaf parsley
pecorino or Parmesan or a blend

Cut the peperoncino in half lengthwise, remove the seeds, and chop. Sauté with garlic cloves, whole and unpeeled or crushed and peeled, in olive oil over medium heat until the garlic is just starting to brown. Add the tomatoes and let simmer for 15 minutes.

Boil the pasta until it is almost fully cooked in salted water and strain. Place the pasta in the pan, increase the flame, and cook everything for a couple of minutes while stirring constantly. Serve right away with chopped parsley and freshly grated pecorino, Parmesan, or half of each.

Spaghetti Vesuvio
Spaghetti with tomato sauce and mozzarella, Campania

2 tbsp olive oil
28–35 oz (800–1000 g) strained tomatoes
1 tsp dried oregano
2 portions of mozzarella (9 oz [250 g])
1.7 oz (50 g) Parmesan
14 oz (400 g) spaghetti

Heat olive oil in a frying pan. Add the strained tomatoes and oregano and let it boil for about 30 minutes. Stir now and then. Dice the mozzarella. Grate the Parmesan.

Boil the pasta until it is almost fully cooked in salted water. Strain and place it in a warm serving bowl. Add and mix the pasta with the ingredients in the following order: first the Parmesan, then the tomato sauce, and lastly the mozzarella on top. Cover with a lid or foil and let it sit for a few minutes so that the cheese melts.

Bucatini all'amatriciana
Bucatini with tomato sauce, Lazio

Bucatini noodles are like thick spaghetti with holes. They are somewhat difficult to cook because it takes a while for them to become flexible, and they are also challenging to eat, because they can't be easily twirled around a fork. The dish originated in Amatrice in northern Lazio. It is a beloved dish in Rome, where it is often served with a more cooperative spaghetti. Sometimes it is served with rigatoni as well.

There is a ongoing debate in Italy as to whether the dish is called *amatriciana* or *matriciana*. In Roman dialect, the first *a* is not pronounced. If you want to take the discussion further, some also claim that the dish is not from Lazio, but from Abruzzo, as Amatrice was once part this neighboring region. The dish is very old and was originally made without tomatoes. The right pork for this is *guanciale*, salted and air-dried pig jowl, a specialty of Lazio. If you can't find *guanciale* then pancetta may be used instead. As a last resort you can also use bacon, but the taste will not be quite the same.

5 oz (150 g) guanciale or pancetta
½ fresh red chili or 1–2 small dried peperoncini, depending on
  potency
3 tbsp olive oil
½–¾ cup (1 ½ dl) dry wine
14 oz (400 g) tomato puree or crushed tomatoes
about 1 lb (500 g) rigatoni
pecorino or Parmesan
flat-leaf parsley (optional)

Finely dice the pork. Cut the chili in half lengthwise, remove the seeds, and mince. Heat some olive oil in a pan and brown the pork and sauté the chili. Add the wine and bring to a simmer. Add tomatoes and return to simmer. Continue to cook until the sauce darkens and thickens.

Boil the pasta in a generous amount of salted water until it is almost done. Strain the pasta then stir in with the sauce. Stir for 1 minute and serve with freshly grated pecorino or Parmesan. Add some chopped parsley on top if desired.

Pasta fresca all'uovo
Basic recipe for fresh pasta

The rule for fresh pasta is 3.5 oz (100 g) flour for every egg. However, eggs vary in size and flour varies in moistness, so you may need to adjust by adding more flour or more liquid (for simplicity's sake you can add water instead of eggs). For four people, ½ lb (200 g) flour and 2 eggs are good measurements to work with. If making sheet pasta for lasagna or cannelloni, you may add some oil to the boiling water to prevent the sheets from sticking together. (This is the only instance in which you should add oil to the water.) The boiling time for fresh pasta is shorter than for dried.

7 oz (200 g) Italian fine wheat flour (00 doppio zero) or
  quality wheat flour
pinch of salt
2 eggs
durum wheat flour for rolling out of the dough (optional)

To make the dough: Sift the flour in a bowl or directly onto a clean countertop with a pinch of salt.

Make a well in the middle of the flour so that it looks like a volcano. Add the eggs to the well. Beat them with a fork then blend the flour in gradually. Continue to work the dough together with your hands. Knead into a ball. If you are not able to work all of the flour in you may add some water. If the dough is too soft, add some flour.

Work the dough for 10 minutes. It should be firm and smooth and should not stick to the countertop. When you press your finger into the dough, it should rise again. If you cut into the dough you should be able to see little pockets of air.

You can also blend the dough by mixing it briefly in a food processor. Place the eggs in the food processor, hit

pulse, and add the flour gradually, hitting pulse a few more times. Knead by hand afterwards until the dough is smooth.

Shape into a ball and let the dough rest for about 20 minutes under a clean kitchen towel or in a covered bowl.

To make the pasta: You can, of course, make pasta with a rolling pin but it can be difficult to roll it out evenly and make it thin enough. It will be significantly easier if you use a pasta machine

Spread parchment paper over the table or countertop where you will be rolling out the pasta. Sprinkle flour on top to prevent the dough from sticking. Sprinkle some flour over the workbench as well. I often use the somewhat harder and rougher durum wheat flour as I find it makes it easier to work with the pasta.

Divide the dough into four equal parts. (A dough made with 6 eggs is divided in three parts, 4 eggs in 8 parts, and so on.) Set the pasta maker to the widest setting then roll out the dough and feed it through the pasta maker. Fold the piece once and feed it through once more. Repeat.

Flat noodles: If you want to make flat noodles such as tagliatelle, continue to feed the remaining pieces through three times as described above before proceeding to the next step. It should be very thin, about 1 mm thick.

Let the sheets dry for 10 minutes before you feed them through the noodle-cutting attachment. If they dry for too long they will become too stiff to feed through the machine.

Attach the noodle-cutting attachment to the machine (see the manual if necessary) then feed the thinly rolled sheet of pasta through, catching the noodles by draping them over your hands once they've passed through the machine.

You can also cut the pasta using a knife. If you choose this method, sprinkle some flour over the sheet of pasta and then fold it inwards on both sides towards the middle. Cut the noodles to the desired width using a sharp knife. Carefully slide the knife under the middle of the noodles

and lift. Place them on a clean kitchen towel—sprinkled with flour and lying on a flat surface—or drape them over something, for instance a kitchen chair, to dry. (Pasta enthusiasts own a special drying rack for this purpose.) Separate the noodles so that they don't stick together.

Continue cutting all of the pasta before cooking it, which should only take a couple of minutes when the time comes. When the pasta has dried completely, it becomes very brittle and will keep for a couple of days.

To make stuffed pasta: Roll out one quarter (or sixth or eighth, depending on quantity prepared) of the dough at a time, keeping the others under a kitchen towel so that that don't dry. Feed the dough through the pasta machine as described above until it is about 1 mm in thickness.

Scoop the filling on top of the sheet of pasta, place another sheet on top, and crimp the edges. Continue with the next portion of dough. Let the finished stuffed pasta lie in one layer on parchment paper covered in flour so that it doesn't stick to the counter.

Pasta fresca di semola di grano duro

Fresh durum wheat pasta

Dried pasta is made with durum wheat flour and water. The harder durum flour can also be used in fresh pasta, which is most commonly made with regular wheat flour. Dough made from durum flour comes out heavier, a tad bit harder to work with, and not as smooth, as durum wheat flour contains less gluten. For the same reason, it is more resistant to heat, which means that a filling won't leak out as easily compared to a pasta made with regular flour.

You can vary the amount of durum flour according to preference and taste, because the flavor and texture of a pasta made with this flour will be different as well.

3.5 oz (100 g) Italian fine wheat flour (00 doppia zero) or quality wheat flour
3.5 oz (100 g) durum wheat flour
1 pinch of salt
2 eggs

Prepare the dough by following the recipe above for pasta with wheat flour.

Agnolotti alla piemontese
Stuffed pasta, Piedmont

1 portion pasta dough (made with 2 eggs)

3.5 oz (100 g) spinach
7 oz (200 g) ricotta
1 oz (30 g) Parmesan
salt
black pepper
nutmeg
6 tbsp (100 g) butter
10 fresh sage leaves
Parmesan for serving

Rinse the fresh spinach and drain. Boil in salted water for 1 minute, then empty into a strainer and hold under cold running water. Drain and squeeze to eliminate excess liquid. As an alternative, you may thaw frozen spinach then squeeze to eliminate excess liquid.

Chop the spinach, then blend with ricotta and freshly grated Parmesan. Season with salt, freshly ground pepper, and nutmeg.

Feed the dough through the pasta machine until it is 1 mm thick. Place it on a lightly floured countertop (I usually use durum wheat for this purpose). Dip a glass in flour and cut circles in the dough. Pick away the leftover dough and work in with the rest of the dough, continuing until you have used all or nearly all of it.

Place small scoops of the spinach, ricotta, and Parmesan blend on the circles. Fold these into a half-moon and squeeze with your fingers along the edges. Make sure that the filling is centered in the middle. Dip a fork in flour and press along the edges to create a seam. Place on a flat surface covered in parchment paper dusted with flour in one layer so that they do not stick together.

Melt butter in a saucepan with the sage leaves. Boil the pasta in lightly salted water (the filling will taste salty) for about 5 minutes. Arrange the angolotti on a serving plate, cover with the sage butter, and serve with freshly grated Parmesan. You may also serve half of the stuffed pasta with tomato sauce.

Mortadella filling:

3.5 oz (100 g) Italian mortadella
7 oz lb (200 g) ricotta
1 oz (30 g) Parmesan
salt
black pepper
nutmeg

Finely chop the mortadella. Blend with ricotta and freshly grated Parmesan. Season with salt, ground black pepper, and grated nutmeg. Make the agnolotti as described above. Serve as above.

Tomato sauce:

1 garlic clove
olive oil
14–18 oz (400–500 g) strained tomatoes
fresh basil (optional)
salt (optional)
black pepper (optional)

Sauté the garlic clove—*in camicia*, with the skin still on, or crushed and peeled—in a saucepan in a generous amount of olive oil until it releases its aroma, but without browning it.

Add the tomatoes and simmer for 30–60 minutes. Stir occasionally. When it is almost ready, the sauce will be dark and thick. If it is too thick, add some water. Add a few basil leaves to the sauce now if desired. You may season with salt and ground back pepper if you like, but it's not necessary. The sauce will taste great just as it is..

Pasta verde
Basic recipe for green pasta

3.5 oz (100 g) spinach
1 ¾ cups (200 g) Italian fine wheat flour, 00 doppio zero, or quality wheat flour
1 pinch of salt
2 eggs

Rinse and drain fresh spinach, then boil in salted water for 1 minute, empty in a strainer and rinse under cold running water. Let the water drain and squeeze to eliminate excess liquids. As an alternative you may thaw frozen spinach then squeeze to eliminate excess liquids as above. Chop the spinach.

Sift the flour in a bowl or directly onto the countertop. Make a well in the middle of the flour like a crater in a volcano. Crack the eggs into the well. Beat the eggs gently with a fork then stir the spinach in with the eggs. Mix the flour in with the spinach and egg blend gradually.

Continue to work the dough with your hands. If you fail to work in all of the flour you may add some water. If the dough is too soft add more flour. Knead the dough for 10 minutes. It should be firm and smooth and should not stick to your hands. When you press your finder into it, the hole should fill out again. If you

cut into the dough you should see little pockets of air. You can also mix the dough in a food processor as long as you knead it by hand until smooth afterwards.

Shape the dough into a ball and let it rest for 20 minutes under a clean kitchen towel or in a covered bowl. You can use this recipe to prepare lasagna or stuffed pasta, or you can cut it into tagliatelle.

Pasta ai pomodori
Tomato pasta

2 ¼ cups (250 g) fine Italian wheat flour (00 doppio zero) or quality wheat flour
1 pinch of salt
2 eggs
1.7 oz (50 g) tomato puree

Prepare the dough by following the basic recipe for fresh pasta but stir the tomato puree in with the eggs at the beginning.

Pasta al nero di seppia
Cuttlefish ink pasta

Ask for squid or cuttlefish ink at your local fish shop, or search the web. You can buy it as a powder as well as in other forms.

2 ¼ cups (250 g) fine Italian wheat flour (00 doppio zero) or quality wheat flour
1 pinch of salt
2 eggs
3 tbsp squid or cuttlefish ink

Prepare the dough by following the basic recipe for fresh pasta, but stir the ink in with the eggs at the beginning..

Pasta alla barbabietola rossa
Red beet pasta

3 oz (80 g) boiled red beets
2 eggs plus 1 yolk
2 ½–¾ cups (300 g) Italian fine wheat flour (00 doppio zero) or quality wheat flour
pinch of salt

Boil the beets until soft. Rinse in cold water and peel the beets using your fingers or a spoon. Cut into smaller pieces and let them cool completely. Mix the beets and eggs in a food processor until smooth. Empty the flour into a bowl, blend with the salt, make a well in the middle, and pour the beet and egg blend into the well. Work this into a dough as in the basic recipe for fresh pasta.

Gnocchi di patate
Potato gnocchi, Piedmont

It is hard to say what the exact measurements should be in this recipe as it depends on the potatoes. Once you've made gnocchi a couple of times you'll get a feel for it. If you use too much flour they will harden; if you use too little flour, there is a risk they will fall apart. The goal is for them to be light and fluffy and not as hard as the store-bought variety.

You can freeze uncooked gnocchi. To do this place them on a floured baking sheet (with some space between them so that they don't stick together) and place in the freezer. When they are frozen, brush away any excess flour and move them into a plastic bag. When the time comes to cook them, boil them without thawing. The boiling time for frozen gnocchi will be a few minutes longer than for fresh ones.

about 1 lb (500 g) slightly mealy potatoes
salt
1 egg
3.5 oz (100 g) wheat flour

Boil the potatoes, unpeeled, in salted water. Peel and mash them while they are still warm. Season with a pinch of salt. Stir in a lightly beaten egg, then the flour.

Work the mixture into a smooth dough that does not stick to your fingers.

Roll out a little of the dough at a time, into cylinders about ⅓ inch (1 cm) thick. Cut these up into ¾ to 1 inch (1 ½–2 cm) long pieces. Press each of these pieces against a fork to create grooves on one side. (The grooves help the gnocchi to pick up the sauce.) Place the finished gnocchi on a clean countertop lined with parchment paper and dusted with flour. Boil one half of the gnocchi in salted water for 3–4 minutes, then the other half.

Serve with a simple tomato sauce or melt butter in a pan with some sage leaves and pour on top. Or serve with a *ragù* like a Neapolitan meat sauce or a sauce made with a sausage base. Serve with freshly grated Parmesan.

Gnocchi verdi
Green gnocchi

7 oz (200 g) fresh leaf spinach or 1–2 oz (50 g) frozen, thawed
salt
1 lb (500 g) mealy potatoes
3.5 oz (100 g) wheat flour
1 egg

Rinse the fresh spinach and drain, then boil it for a couple of minutes. Strain and cool. Squeeze to eliminate excess liquids and then chop finely. Prepare the gnocchi dough as described above. Stir in the chopped spinach. Add more flour if the dough is too soft.

Gorgonzola sauce:

3 tbsp (50 g) butter
1.7 oz (50 g) gorgonzola
whipping cream
salt
black pepper
Parmesan

Melt butter is a saucepan. Cut the gorgonzola into small pieces and stir in with the butter until the gorgonzola melts. Add whipping cream and continue to cook until the sauce is well blended and fairly thick. Add the boiled gnocchi to the sauce and stir. Season with salt and fresh ground black pepper. Serve with grated Parmesan.

Gnocchi alla romana
Roman-style gnocchi, Lazio

This dish is often made with a rougher *semolina*, but you can also make it with the regular fine *semolina*, durum wheat. The original Roman recipe is made with regular wheat flour. The variety with *semolina* is from Piedmont but is common enough in Rome that they adopted it.

4 cups (1 liter) milk
nutmeg
salt
black pepper
½ lb (250 g) durum wheat
6 tbsp (100 g) butter
9 oz (250 g) pecorino Romano or Parmesan
3 egg yolks
olive oil

Heat milk with a dash of grated nutmeg, salt, and freshly ground pepper in a saucepan. Do not allow mixture to boil. Add the flour a little at a time, whisking it well so that there are no lumps. When it has begun to thicken you can switch to a wooden spoon. Continue stirring until it is no longer sticking to the sides of the saucepan, about 15 minutes. Add 5 tablespoons (75 g) butter while stirring and work it in with the blend.

Remove the saucepan from the stove and stir in 5 oz (150 g) pecorino Romano or Parmesan. Add the yolks.

Grease a baking pan with olive oil and spread the blend out about ⅓ inch (1 cm) thick. Let stiffen. Place in the fridge, when it cools it stiffens more quickly.

Cut in about 1 ½ inch (4 cm) squares or make rounds with a glass or a round cookie cutter. Place on parchment paper on a baking sheet. Add the rest of the butter and grated cheese on top. Set the oven to grill on the highest setting. Grill to a nice color.

Malfatti
Ricotta gnocchi with spinach, Lombardy

The name means "poorly done" and refers to how they look like smeared ravioli fill. Also called *gnocchi verdi*.

14 oz (400 g) frozen spinach, thawed
½ lb (250 g) ricotta
2 yolks
1.7 oz (50 g) Parmesan
salt
black pepper
nutmeg
wheat flour
⅓ cup (75 g) butter
fresh sage leaves
Parmesan

Rinse, drain, and squeeze the spinach well. Chop the leaves. Blend ricotta, yolk, freshly grated Parmesan, and spinach. Season with salt, freshly ground black pepper, and some grated nutmeg. Shape into oval, walnut-sized balls. Dredge lightly in flour. Boil in salted water for 3–4 minutes.

Melt butter in a saucepan with sage leaves. Pour over the *malfatti* before serving and top it off with some grated Parmesan.

RISO e POLENTA
rice & polenta

Rice dishes are served as *primi piatti* and are associated with northern Italy. Rice was most likely brought to Sicily by the Arabs in the eighth or ninth century. Large-scale cultivation of rice in northern Italy began around the River Po as late as the late nineteenth century

Today, Italy is Europe's largest manufacturer of rice. You find rice dishes all over Italy, but they are most significant to northern Italian cuisine. In Piedmont, Lombardy, and Veneto, rice is traditionally more important than pasta.

The varieties *carnaroli* and *vialone nano* are the best for making risotto. *Arborio* rice also works well, but the risotto will not be as creamy. Do not rinse the rice before preparation.

Some people like their risotto firmer, others creamier. In Venice, they like it *all'onda*, with a wave, meaning that a little wave forms when you shake the saucepan or plate. Whenever possible, risotto should be served right away. If it is left to sit for too long it will become much firmer. It's not a good idea to prepare risotto in advance and heat before serving; however, you can cook it halfway and continue later when it's closer to serving time.

Polenta is typical of the north, but similar dishes are made in the south as well, where they are often made with chili. They are served as *primi* or as *contorni* (side dishes) to accompany the *secondo piatti*.

Corn gained popularity in northern Italy during the eighteenth century when the Habsburgs controlled the area. They introduced corn as a solution to widespread hunger and poverty.

Risotto al Barolo
Risotto with Barolo wine, Piedmont

4 cups (1 liter) chicken or beef stock
4 tbsp butter
1 bay leaf
1 yellow onion
½ lb (300 g) risotto rice
1 ¼ cups (2 ½ dl) Barolo wine or other rich Italian red wine
1.7 oz (50 g) Parmesan
salt
black pepper

Bring the stock to a boil. In a separate saucepan, melt half of the butter, then add the bay leaf.

Finely chop the onion and sauté until soft in the saucepan. Add the rice and sauté while stirring.

Add the wine and let the mixture simmer. Pour in just enough stock to cover the rice. Let it simmer while stirring constantly. Add more stock as needed. There should be a little liquid surrounding the rice and it should never be exposed while it is cooking. Continue to cook the rice until it is al dente.

Grate the Parmesan and stir into the pan with the butter. Adjust the texture with more stock or hot water if needed.

Remove the saucepan from the stove. Season with salt and ground black pepper. Serve.

Risotto alla Milanese
Milan-style risotto with saffron, Lombardy

This classic risotto from Milan is usually served with ossobuco. It's hard to say exactly where the saffron in this recipe comes from, as it's not common in Lombardy. It might be part of the region's luxurious renaissance heritage, in which case it could date back to when the Sforza family ruled Milan, or it may have been inspired by the famous glass master *Zafferno*, who was known for his plentiful use of saffron when he colored the glass for the Duomo in Milan.

A real *Milanese* should also contain bone marrow, but you can skip this if it seems complicated, or substitute with red wine..

6 cups (1 ½) liter chicken or meat stock
⅓ cup (80 g) butter
0.7 oz (20 g) bone marrow or ½ cup (1 dl) dry red wine
1 small yellow onion
12 oz (350 g) risotto rice
1 pinch (½–1 g) saffron
salt
black pepper
2.5 oz (75 g) Parmesan

Bring the stock to a boil. Melt half of the butter in a saucepan. If using marrow, add to the skillet and sauté in the butter.

Finely chop the onion and sauté until soft. Add the rice and sauté while stirring until the grains become glossy. If you wish to add wine, pour in the pan and bring to a simmer.

Cover the rice with hot stock and let simmer while stirring. Add more stock if needed. It should always be somewhat runny and it should never be dry while cooking. It takes about 20 minutes to cook the rice. When there are about 5 minutes to go, stir in the saffron. Boil the rice until it is al dente. Season with salt and freshly ground black pepper.

Remove the pan from the stove. Stir in the rest of the butter and freshly grated Parmesan..

Risotto al radicchio e taleggio
Risotto with radicchio and taleggio, Lombardy

Radicchio is a bitter red lettuce, though it is not technically a lettuce but a member of the endive family. There are various kinds: a round one from Verona and from Treviso an elongated variety that resembles an endive and one with long curly leaves.

6 cups (1 ½ liters) chicken stock
1 yellow onion
butter and/or olive oil
1 head radicchio
½ lb (300 g) risotto rice
¾ cup (1 ½ dl) dry white wine
4.5 oz (125 g) taleggio
salt
black pepper

Bring the stock to a boil. Finely chop the onion and sauté in butter and/or olive oil until soft.

Cut the radicchio and remove the hard stalk. Shred the radicchio and sauté with the onion until soft. Add the rice and sauté until every grain of rice is glossy from the butter and oil. Add the wine and bring to a boil while stirring constantly. Cover the rice with stock. Simmer while stirring. Add more bouillon if needed. The rice should always be a little runny and it should never be dry while cooking.

If you run out of stock while cooking, add hot water. Remove the pan from the stove when the rice is al dente.

Cut the rind of the cheese off and dice. Add to the risotto and stir until it is completely melted. Season with salt and freshly ground pepper. Serve.

Risotto alle fragole
Risotto with strawberries, Piedmont

For most, strawberries are associated with desserts, but here they provide taste to a summery dish.

6 cups (1 ½ liter) vegetable stock
1 small yellow onion
⅓ cup (100 g) butter
12 oz (350 g) risotto rice
1 ¾ cups (3 ½ dl) dry white wine
8 oz (300 g) strawberries
1 ¼ cups (2 ½ dl) cream
salt
black pepper

Bring the stock to a boil. Finely chop the onion. Heat half of the butter in a saucepan and sauté the onion until soft.

Add the rice and sauté, stirring until every grain of rice is glossy from the butter. Add the wine and bring to a simmer.

Cover the rice with hot stock. Simmer while stirring. Add more stock if needed. It should always be a little runny; the rice should never be dry while cooking.

Set some strawberries aside for the garnish. Mash the others and add to the risotto after half the boiling time, or when 7–10 minutes have elapsed.

When the rice is al dente remove from the heat and add the cream. Season with salt and black pepper. Garnish with strawberries and serve.

Risotto ai gamberi
Risotto with shrimp, Veneto

Risotto made with shellfish or fish will usually be served without cheese. Make the stock weaker if you use precooked shrimp, since they are already salted; otherwise, there's a risk the dish will be to salty.

¾ (1 ½ dl) dry white wine
1 bay leaf
salt
½ lb (200 g) shrimp, peeled
1 small yellow onion
2 tbsp olive oil
1 garlic clove
12 oz (350 g) risotto rice
4 cups (1 liter) stock
leaf parsley
black pepper

Boil the wine and 1 ¼ cups (2 ½ dl) water with the bay leaf and salt.

If using raw shrimp, let them boil for a couple of minutes in a separate saucepan. Frozen or fresh shrimp are placed directly in the boiling wine and water and are later strained. Save both the liquid and the shrimp.

Finely chop the onion and sauté until soft in a saucepan with some olive oil. Finely chop the garlic and sauté until soft as well.

Add the rice and sauté while stirring until the grains are glossy from the oil.

Cover the rice with the hot water from the shrimp and simmer while stirring. Add more water if needed. The rice should always be somewhat wet; it should never be dry while cooking. Use hot stock for this purpose when the water the shrimp were boiled in is finished.

Remove the saucepan from the stove when the rice is al dente. Stir in the shrimp and finely chopped parsley. Season with salt and freshly ground black pepper.

Risotto con pancetta e salvia
Risotto with pancetta and sage, Lombardy

6 cups (1 ½ liter) chicken stock
5 oz (150 g) pancetta
4 tbsp butter
1 large yellow onion
½ lb (300 g) risotto rice
1 handful fresh sage leaves
1.7 oz (50 g) Parmesan
black pepper
salt (optional)

Bring the stock to a boil. Dice the pancetta and sauté in some butter in a separate saucepan until the pancetta releases its fat. Finely chop the onion and sauté until soft. Add the rice and sauté while stirring until every grain is glossy from the fat.

Cover the rice with stock and bring to a simmer. Let it simmer, stirring constantly. Add more stock if needed. There should always be liquid in the saucepan; the rice should never be dry while cooking.

Finely chop the sage and simmer with the rest.

When the rice is ready—some like it cooked all the way though, others prefer it al dente with a small, uncooked core at the center of each grain—add the freshly grated Parmesan and the remaining butter. Season with freshly ground black pepper and salt if desired.

Risotto alla sarda
Risotto with ground meat, Sardinia

If you are unable to find ground veal for use in this recipe, you can also use mixed ground meat or pork.

4 cups (1 liter) beef stock
1 small yellow onion
6 tbsp olive oil
5 oz (150 g) ground veal
5 oz (150 g) ground pork
½ lb (300 g) risotto rice
3 tbsp dry red wine
½ lb (200 g) tomato puree or crushed tomatoes
1 pinch (½ g) saffron
2 ½ tbsp. (40 g) butter
2 oz (60 g) pecorino
salt
black pepper

Bring the stock to a boil. Finely chop the onion and sauté in some olive oil in a separate saucepan until soft. Brown the meat while stirring. Add the rice and sauté while stirring until each grain is glossy from the oil. Add the wine and bring to a simmer.

Add tomatoes, saffron, and enough stock to cover the rice. Let simmer while stirring. Add more stock if needed. There should always be liquid in the saucepan; the rice should never be dry while cooking. Cook until the rice is al dente.

Remove the saucepan from the stove and stir in the butter and freshly grated pecorino. Adjust the texture with more stock if needed. Season with salt and pepper. Serve.

Risotto al limone
Risotto with lemon, Sicily

This risotto is richer with cheese (use either *caciocavallo* or Parmesan). Without cheese, it is lighter and more delicate.

4 cups (1 liter) light stock, either meat or vegetable
juice and zest of 1 lemon
1 small yellow onion
1 oz (30 g) butter
12 oz (350 g) risotto rice
½ cup (1 dl) dry white wine
flat-leaf parsley
salt
black pepper
1.7 oz (50 g) caciocavallo or Parmesan (optional)

Bring the stock to a boil. Juice and grate the zest of the lemon. Set juice and zest aside.

Finely chop the onion and sauté until soft in a separate saucepan. Add the rice and sauté while stirring until each grain is glossy. Add half of the lemon zest along with the wine and bring to a simmer.

Cover the rice with the hot stock and let it simmer while stirring it constantly. Add more stock when needed. There should always be liquid in the saucepan; the rice should never be dry while cooking. It will take about 15–20 minutes for the rice to cook.

When the rice is al dente, remove the saucepan from the stove and stir in finely chopped parsley, the remaining lemon zest, and lemon juice. Season with salt and freshly ground pepper. Stir in freshly grated cheese if including, or serve separately.

Risotto ai funghi
Risotto with mushrooms, Piedmont

Make this with wild mushrooms or the Italian favorite, porcini. Dried mushrooms are fine as well. If you buy dried porcini, 1 oz (30 g) is equal to about ½ lb (250 g) fresh mushrooms.

Let the dried mushrooms soak in lukewarm water for about 15 minutes. Save the water you soak the mushrooms in to add to the stock.

1 liter light stock, vegetable, chicken, or beef
½ lb (200 g) mushrooms, cleaned and trimmed
3 tbsp butter
salt
black pepper
1 yellow onion
12 oz (350 g) risotto rice
2 garlic cloves
1 handful flat-leaf parsley
1.7 oz (50 g) Parmesan

Bring the stock to a boil. Cut up the mushrooms. Sauté in half of the butter. Season with salt and freshly ground black pepper.

Finely chop the onion and sauté in the remaining butter in a separate pan. Sauté until soft. Stir in the rice and sauté until every grain is glossy.

Cover the rice with hot stock and simmer while stirring constantly. Add more stock if needed. There should always be liquid in the saucepan; the rice should never be dry while cooking.

Finely chop garlic and parsley. Add mushrooms, garlic, and parsley when the rice has boiled for 10 minutes.

Remove the pan from the stove when the rice is al dente. Stir in freshly grated Parmesan. Adjust with more hot stock or hot water if needed.

Season with salt and freshly ground pepper. Serve.

Risotto con asparagi
Asparagus risotto, Veneto

When asparagus is in season you can find it all over Italy, but it is a particular favorite in Venice.

6 cups (1 ½ liter) vegetable stock
1 lb (500 g) green asparagus
2 oz (65 g) butter
1 small yellow onion
2 tbsp olive oil
12 oz (350 g) risotto rice
¾ cup (1 ½ dl) dry white wine
1.7 oz (50 g) Parmesan
salt
black pepper

Bring the stock to a boil. Snap off the bottoms of the asparagus stalks. To do this, simply bend the asparagus and let it break wherever it breaks naturally. Discard the bottoms.

Place the asparagus in a pot, cover with salted water, and boil. They should be tender but not too soft. To test doneness, poke the stem near the bottom of the asparagus with a fork; the fork should enter with little resistance. Drain the asparagus and save the boiling water. Rinse them in cold water. Cut the tips off. Sauté them carefully in a couple of tablespoons of butter. Set aside.

Finely chop the onion and sauté in olive oil and some butter until soft. Add the rice and sauté while stirring until every rice grain is glossy from the fat.

Finely chop the rest of the asparagus and add to the pan as well. Add the wine and bring to a simmer. Add some of the water you boiled the asparagus in to the stock.

Cover the rice with stock and simmer while stirring. Add more stock if needed. There should always be liquid in the saucepan; the rice should never be dry while cooking.

Remove the saucepan from the stove when the rice is al dente. Stir in the grated Parmesan, the remaining butter, and asparagus tips and serve.

Polenta

Polenta is a rough cornmeal. There are two varieties, the finer pale yellow variety from Veneto and the coarser variety from Lombardy and Piedmont. The polenta from Venice is usually served soft, *all'onda*, so that a wave appears when you shake the plate, as with creamy mashed potatoes. They usually serve this with fish. The coarser variety is prepared firm with a pudding-like texture.

Before corn came to Italy, they made similar dishes with legumes, like the Etruscan pulse and the Roman *pulmentum*. Corn came to Venice from Turkey during the 1500s and was called grano turco.

Real polenta takes anywhere from 45 minutes to several hours to prepare. The longer the polenta boils, the easier it is said to digest. Pre-cooked polenta doesn't take long at all to prepare, but it doesn't taste as good.

4 cups (8 dl) water, or half water and half milk
1 bay leaf
1 tsp salt
5 oz (150 g) polenta
4.4 oz (125 g) gorgonzola, fontina or Parmesan (optional)

Loose polenta: Bring water or water and milk to a boil with the bay leaf and salt in a large saucepan—you will need a lot of room, as the polenta will rise significantly.

Add the polenta while stirring to avoid lumps. Simmer while stirring constantly for at least 45 minutes. The polenta will burn if you don't stir. Add hot water as needed.

When ready, the polenta should pull away from the sides of the pan and have the texture of fluffy mashed potatoes.

Serve as is, or stir in a few tablespoons of butter.

If you like, you can stir in diced gorgonzola, fontina, or freshly grated Parmesan while it's still hot. Herbs and tomato sauce are also good options.

For firm polenta, pour into a glass or metal dish and let cool for at least 1–1 ½ hours.

To make polenta *fritta*, cut firm polenta into pieces and fry until golden brown. Or brush with olive oil and spice with herbs and cook on a grill, grill pan or in the oven, for *crostini di polenta*.

Either may be served as a side for meat or fish. The grilled variety is usually served as *antipasto* and is used as *crostini* with fried mushrooms or other toppings

You can also slice the polenta thin and layer it with *ragù*, mushrooms, cheese, or sausages and a cheese sauce or béchamel sauce.

CARNE e POLLO *meat & chicken*

Italians are not great meat-eaters. This is in partly because of the poverty in Italy's past. For a long time, many people simply couldn't afford to eat their animals, and most people did not own the land they needed to raise large numbers of animals. Land was first and foremost for cultivating grapes for wine, olives, and fruits and vegetables.

Meat is served as a *secondo piatto, or secondo*. An entire meal will often consist of multiple vegetable dishes. The vegetables can dominate both the *antipasto* and *primo piatto* courses. When a small meat dish is then served, one or more vegetable side dishes, *contorni*, often accompany it. These are served on separate plates.

Meat is often sliced thinly, cooked briefly on a griddle, and served with lemon, or used to prepare a stew. Italians love their pork and have recipes that make use of every single part. Veal is also very popular. Lamb, wild boar, and rabbit are also common. Chicken dishes are often quick and simple. Other kinds of poultry used to be more common in Italian cuisine, but today the chicken has in large part replaced them.

Cotoletta alla Milanese
Breaded veal cutlet

Do not even *think* about calling this a Milan-style wiener schnitzel; this will only lead to an hour-long monologue about how the Milanese originated the dish and the Viennese copied it. Besides, the *costoletta alla milanese* is breaded only once while the wiener schnitzel is breaded twice.

1 lb (500 g) veal cutlet
bread crumbs
2 eggs
salt
black pepper
4 tbsp butter
1 lemon

Cover the meat with plastic wrap and gently pound it thin using a meat tenderizer or rolling pin.

Empty a generous amount of bread crumbs into a shallow bowl or pan. In a separate bowl, crack the eggs, season with salt and black pepper, and whisk lightly. Dredge the meat in the bread crumbs, then the eggs, and then the bread crumbs once more. Place on a drying rack and let dry for 10 minutes.

Melt the butter in a skillet. Fry the cutlets until golden brown, about 3–4 minutes on each side. Serve with lemon wedges.

Scaloppina al limone
Veal cutlet with lemon, Lombardy

1 lb (500 g) veal cutlet
flour
salt
black pepper
zest and juice of 1 lemon
4 tbsp olive oil
4 tbsp butter
½ cup (1 dl) dry white wine
flat-leaf parsley
lemon slices

Cover the meat with plastic wrap and gently pound until thin using a meat tenderizer or rolling pin. Cut into 10–12 cm wide pieces. Dredge in flour so that they are thinly coated. Season with salt and freshly ground pepper. Grate the lemon zest, taking care to avoid the pith. Feel free to use a potato peeler to create nice-looking spirals.

Heat olive oil and 2 tbsp butter in a large skillet. Fry the cutlets until golden brown, about 1 minute on each side. Place the meat on a plate.

Deglaze pan by bringing wine, lemon juice, and lemon zest to a simmer in the pan and cooking for about 1 minute. Melt the remaining 2 tbsp of butter in the pan and return the meat to the pan. Decorate with chopped parsley and lemon slices and serve..

Saltimbocca alla romana
Veal cutlet with prosciutto and sage, Lazio

Amazingly simple, quick, and so tasty, this dish can also be made with pork or chicken cutlets. The combination of prosciutto di Parma and sage is also great with fish. Remember that veal cutlets cook quickly, so wait until everything else you are serving is ready before finishing this dish.

1 lb (500 g) veal cutlet
3.5 oz (100 g) prosciutto di Parma
8-10 fresh sage leaves
3 tbsp (50 g) butter
salt
black pepper
½ cup (1 dl) dry wine

Cover the meat with plastic wrap and carefully pound it until thin using a meat tenderizer or rolling pin. Place prosciutto di Parma on top. Cut into 4 to 5 inch (10–12 cm) strips. Smaller pieces look nicer and are easier to deal with.

Fasten a large sage leaf (or two smaller ones) on top of each piece using a toothpick. Melt butter in a pan. Place the cutlets with the prosciutto di Parma facing down. Cook until golden brown. Flip and brown on the other side. Season with salt and black pepper.

Because the meat is thin, the pan needs to be very hot in order for the meat to brown before it cooks all the way through. Fry in two batches to make sure that the pan doesn't cool down from contact with the meat. Place the cooked veal on a plate.

When everything is cooked, lower the heat and pour the wine in the pan to deglase. Let it simmer for a while so that the drippings blend with the wine. Add a half tablespoon or so of butter. Return all of the cutlets to the pan to warm. Turn so that the wine and heat are evenly distributed. Serve right away.

Involtini di vitello
Veal roulades, Sicily

Veal roulades are served all over Sicily, with crispy breading, fried or grilled, and with various fillings. A simple sauce is delicious with breaded roulades. If you do not bread the roulade you can also serve it with a simple tomato sauce.

14 oz (400 g) veal cutlet, sirloin or topside

Filling:
125 caciocavallo, fontina, or mozzarella
¾ cup (1 ½ dl) flat-leaf parsley
¾ cup (1 ½ dl) freshly grated Parmesan or pecorino
1 egg
salt
black pepper
½ small garlic clove (optional)

Breading:
1 egg
1 tbsp water
bread crumbs
butter and oil for frying

¾ cup (1 ½ dl) dry white wine
½ lemon, cut into thin slices
juice of ½ lemon

You can ask the butcher to pound the cutlets for you—the thinner the better. Be careful when you pound them yourself that you don't break them down so much that holes form. Hold the meat in place while you pound it so that the meat is stretched out and becomes thinner. Cut the meat into elongated pieces measuring about 2 ½ by 4 inches (6 x 10 cm).

Sicialians use *caciocavallo*, a pear-shaped cheese. You can also use north Italy's fontina or mozzarella. Dice the cheese.

Finely chop the parsley. Mix the caciocavallo (or fontina or mozzarella), parsley, Parmesan or pecorino, and egg to create the filling. Season with salt and freshly ground pepper. Also flavor with some grated or crushed garlic.
Place some of the filling close to the end of the meat and roll up to form roulades. Fasten in place with a toothpick.

Whisk eggs and water lightly. Dip the roulades in the egg mixture then dredge in bread crumbs. Let dry. Fry until golden brown in butter and olive or canola oil over medium heat. Place the roulades on a plate.

Let wine, lemon slices, and lemon juice simmer together quickly in the pan to deglaze it. Place the roulade in the pan and cook briefly. Serve as is or with a vegetable side. We also recommend a good bread to absorb the last of the broth.

Alternate filling:
2–3 tbsp raisins
2–3 tbsp pine nuts
salami, boiled ham, and/or mortadella

Alternate sauce:

1–2 garlic cloves
3 tbsp olive oil
1 lb (500 g) tomatoes puree
¼ cup (½ dl) red wine (optional)
fresh basil leaves (optional)

Cutlets that are not breaded are browned in butter and oil. They can also be grilled. The breaded cutlets can be grilled as well and if necessary may finish cooking in an oven set at a low temperature, 250–300 degrees (125–150 C).

You can use everything or just one ingredient from the alternate filling for variation. If you add finely chopped salami or ham, you can use less of the pecorino or Parmesan. If you are making the tomato sauce it is wise to begin this right away, because the longer it simmers the better it will taste.

Sauce: Sauté whole unpeeled garlic cloves *(in camicia)* in olive oil until they release their aroma. Do not let them brown. Remove and discard or leave them in and let them cook with the sauce.

Add tomato puree and simmer for 30–60 minutes. You can season in the beginning with red wine and/or basil. Add water if the sauce is too thick. Let the roulades cook with the sauce for a while before serving.

Arista alla fiorentina
Roasted pork loin, Tuscany

In 1439, there was a church meeting in Florence. Pork loin spiced with garlic and rosemary was served and was very well received by the Greek bishops. They exclaimed "Aristis!" meaning excellent, or the best. Ideally, the loin should roast on a skewer, but a roasting pan works just fine. You can also buy *Arista* cured; it is sliced thinly and eaten cold.

2.2 lb (1 kg) boneless pork loin
3 garlic cloves
3 springs rosemary
zest of 1 lemon
1 tsp fennel seeds
1 pinch ground carnation spice
salt
black pepper
olive oil
beef broth
potatoes

Preheat the oven to 350 F (175 C).

Peel and mince the garlic. Finely chop the rosemary. Rinse the lemon and grate the zest, taking care not to grate the pith.

Blend garlic and an equal amount of rosemary (save the rest) with lemon zest, fennel seeds, carnation spice, salt and ground black pepper—preferably in a mortar so that they are worked together into a paste when the garlic is crushed.

Cut slits 1/3 inch (1 cm) deep with a knife all around the loin. Stick a pinch of the spice blend in each slit. Salt and pepper the meat. Take the rest of the rosemary and pat it all around the outside of the meat to form something like a crust. Tie with kitchen string so that the loin maintains its shape. Pat with olive oil.

Stick an oven thermometer in the center of the loin. Place in a baking dish and place in the oven. Roast until the inside temperature has reached 150 F (65 C) degrees, about 1–1 ½ hours. Ladle some of the broth over the meat now and then.

When the loin has begun to release liquid, dice potatoes and arrange then around the meat in the baking dish. Rotate them now and then so that they cook evenly and become golden on all sides.

To mimic cooking on a skewer, you can place the loin on a metal rack inside the pan, turning it now and then so that it cooks evenly on all sides.

Let the loin rest for 10 minutes before cutting and serving.

Porchetta alla romana
Pork belly with herbs and wine, Lazio

As we've said, Italians love their pork, and roasted piglets stuffed with herbs are popular in many parts of the country. They are prepared with mixed herbs in Marche, rosemary and garlic in Rome, fennel seeds and garlic in Umbria, sage and garlic in Tuscany.

At the markets in Tuscany, Abruzzo, Lazio, Marche, and Umbria there are food trucks serving *porchetta*, slices of moist, savory pork in sandwiches.

You *can't* roast an entire pig at home every day, but you can make *porchetta* in your home kitchen. You simply create a rub for the pork belly or a boneless pork loin that's been cut almost all the way through and then folded like a book so that you get a large, rather thin piece of meat. Later, the meat is rolled together and cooked on a skewer.

3.3 lb (1 ½ kg) pork belly or boneless pork loin
4 garlic cloves
4 large sage leaves
1 spring rosemary
2 tbsp fennel seeds
½ tsp freshly ground nutmeg
olive oil
salt
black pepper
1 ¼ cup (2 ½ dl) dry white wine

Set the oven to 300 F (150 C).

Cut a checkered pattern in the fat on the skin side of the pork belly. Place it with the skin side facing up in a sink and pour boiling hot water over it. As a result, the skin will pull together and get a nice crust later on.

Peel and finely chop the garlic cloves. Finely chop sage; you should have the same amount of sage as garlic. Finely chop an equal amount of rosemary as well. Blend with the fennel seeds, nutmeg, and enough oil that it holds together, almost like a paste.

Place the pork belly with the skin side facing down. Rub salt and freshly ground pepper over the meat. Rub evenly with the spice blend.

Roll the meat tightly together and tie with kitchen string. Pat the outside with olive oil.

Place the meat in a baking dish and add the wine. Roast in the oven for about 1 ½ hours. Scoop the drippings and wine over the meat now and then. Remove from the oven and let it rest for 10 minutes before cutting and serving.

Ragù alla napoletana
Meat stew from Naples, Campania

This is traditional Sunday supper fare in Naples. Neapolitans will set the stew on the stove in early morning and go out for mass. By the time they return, it's ready to be eaten.

You can make two dishes out of this. First, a *primo*, a pasta dish where a short, thick, dried pasta is blended with the tomato sauce in the stew and served with grated Parmesan or pecorino; then, a *secondo* in which the meat is served on its own, with a *contorno*, a vegetable side dish, on a separate plate, perhaps a *parmigiana di melanzane*—eggplant Parmesan—or something similar.

You can make *ragù* with just meat, garlic, basil, and tomato puree if you like, but other ingredients often accompany them, especially yellow onion, celery, and carrot—in other words, a classic *soffrito*. A piece of bread, familiarly known as *una scarpetta*—literally, a little shoe—is needed to soak up the last of the delicious sauce from the plate.

2 garlic cloves
6 tbsp olive oil
1 lb (500 g) prime rib of veal
1 yellow onion
1 celery stalk
1 carrot
8 cups (2 liters) tomato puree
1 handful basil leaves
salt
black pepper

Crush the garlic cloves and sauté until soft in olive oil in a Dutch oven or stockpot. Remove the garlic from the pot and discard.

Cut the meat into large cubes, add to the pot, and brown it in two batches. If you add too much meat at a time the pan will cool and the meat will be boiled instead of browning. Remove the meat and set aside. Finely chop yellow onion. Dice celery and carrot. Sauté yellow onion until soft, then add the celery and carrot and sauté for a few minutes more. Return the meat to the pot. Add tomato puree and basil leaves and let simmer for a few hours, stirring occasionally.

Dilute with water if the sauce is too thick. Add more basil leaves if desired. Season with salt and freshly ground pepper.

Salsiccia con lenticchie
Salsiccia with lentils, Umbria

This dish from Norcia is made with lentils from Castelluccio, a small town a couple of miles away, but you may also use another kind of small green lentils that you don't have to soak, such as Puy lentils. (These lentils also work as a nice complement to grilled meat.)

1.7 oz (50 g) pancetta or smoked pork belly
olive oil
1 small yellow onion
2 celery stalks
2 garlic cloves
½ lb (300 g) small green lentils
salt
black pepper
4 large or 8 small salsiccia (sausages)

If soaking the lentils, cover them with cold water and set aside several hours before beginning, or even the night before.

Dice the pancetta or pork belly finely. Sauté in olive oil until it releases its fat. Finely chop yellow onion. Dice celery. Sauté the yellow onion until soft. Add the celery and let it sauté with the onion for a few minutes. Finely chop the garlic and let sauté with the others for a couple of minutes more.

Rinse the lentils and drain. Add the lentils to the pan and cover with water. Simmer the lentils until they are soft, about 20–25 minutes. Add more water if needed. Season with salt and freshly ground black pepper.

Poke the sausages with a sharp knife to prevent the skin from breaking. Sauté the sausages in some olive oil over medium heat until they have a nice color all over. Arrange the lentils on plates, top with sausages, and serve.

105

Adriano Birro

"THE SIXTIES WERE CHALLENGING," SAYS ADRIANO.
They had Italian week at the store: "Make your own pizza on hönökaka (Swedish bread) with ketchup and squeezy cheese. If you added sliced fish cakes it was a *Marinara*. With shredded sausage and champignons it became a *capricciosa*."

Adriano Birro is from the city Noventa Vicentia, a few miles south of Vicenza in Veneto. He grew up with his mother and four sisters. When his sisters married and Adriano was a teenager, he and his mother moved to Turin, the capital of Piedmont. After high school he worked at a business that made lithographs the traditional way and later at a factory that SFK (the Swedish rolling bearing company) had bought. Adriano was one of 40 workers that went to Sweden to learn how to work the SFK way.

"It was a culture shock. The bread was sweet, the preserved vegetables were sweet. There were peas and carrots in a can. I came in 1964 and broke my contract in 1965 to return home."

But Adriano had met Eva in Sweden. In summer, she came down to Turin. Adriano did not want to go back to Sweden, so Eva went on her own.

"Then I lost my job, and I missed her as well."
So he ended up in Sweden after all, with a job in healthcare and two sons, Peter and Marcus.

EVERY SUMMER THE FAMILY DROVE down to Italy and visited relatives. But nurturing the Italian side of their heritage did not come naturally to his sons.

"For a while they were into punk culture and went to London a lot," Adriano tells us. I didn't say anything but . . . With time, they have come into touch with their Italian identities."

Marcus nurtures a passion for Italian soccer and Peter and his Italian wife split their time between Rome and Sweden.

"The food I eat comes from multiple regions," says Adriano. "But, if I am to be totally honest, Tuscan food is my favorite."

"I was certainly no chef, but I married a Swede who couldn't cook. We were both happy when I started learning. She was happy because now she didn't have to cook, and I was happy because I got to eat Italian food. I often called Italy to ask for advice.

"But Swedish culture and cuisine are also exciting. It is valuable to be part of two cultures."

Fegato alla veneziana
Venice-style veal liver

This is a traditional dish in Veneto. When you allow the onion to sauté slowly on low heat it becomes sweet. "When I used to call my sister to ask how to cook certain dishes I never received an actual recipe," Adriano says. "It was more about intuition and flavors. How much should there be of one or the other? There's really no answer to that. You judge based on how it tastes. Whenever I asked her for a measurement, she just responded *'quanto basta'*—however much is enough."

1 lb (500 g) yellow onion
4–5 tbsp olive oil
2 tbsp butter
1 lb (500 g) veal liver
salt
black pepper
¾ cup (1 ½ dl) dry white wine
½ cup (1 dl) veal stock
generous amounts of flat-leaf parsley

Slice the onion thinly. Heat olive oil and butter in a pan and sauté until it is soft, translucent, and sweet, about 10 minutes, stirring occasionally. Take care not to let it brown. You can cover the pan if you wish.

Remove the onion. Thinly slice the liver—or have the butcher slice it for you—then cut into shreds.

Brown the liver over medium heat, stirring occasionally, until it takes on a golden color; this should take a few minutes. Season with salt and pepper. Brown the liver pieces in two batches so that the pan doesn't cool down as a result of contact with the meat.

Remove the liver pieces from the pan and set aside. Add the wine and bring to a simmer to deglaze the pan. Return the onion and liver to the pan, then add the stock. Heat everything, stirring constantly.

Stir in chopped parsley and arrange on serving plates. Serve with grilled polenta (see page 90).

Adriano Birro is father of the Brothers Birro, as they are known in Sweden: Peter, an actor and writer, and Marcus, an author and media personality. Adriano is divorced and lives in a shared house where they serve common dinners at least twice a week. He is known as a talented cook.

Polpette alla napoletana
Naples-style meatballs, Campania

Before you think of *Lady and the Tramp*, remember that meatballs are *not* served with spaghetti in Naples (although you can find them served this way in Apulia). However, the sauce they cook the meatballs in may be served separately with pasta as a *primo*. The meatballs are eaten afterwards as *secondo*, without sauce, but accompanied by a vegetable side dish. In Naples, they also like to stick *polpette* in various oven-baked dishes. In that case, they tend to be somewhat smaller.

¼ cup (½ dl) raisins
1 lb (500 g) veal, pork, or mixed ground meat
3.5 oz (100 g) pecorino
3.5 oz (100 g) bread crumbs from fresh bread
¾ cup (1 ½ dl) chopped flat-leaf parsley
¼ cup (½ dl) pine nuts
1 tsp salt
black pepper
2 eggs
wheat flour
olive oil
1–2 garlic cloves
0.8-1 lb (400–500 g) tomato puree

Soak the raisins for 15 minutes.

Squeeze and place in a bowl with ground meat, freshly grated pecorino, fresh bread crumbs (*see Polpette al limone*), parsley, pine nuts, salt, freshly ground black pepper, and eggs. Blend well.

Shape into plum-sized balls. Dredge in flour, brushing away any excess flour. Heat a few tablespoons of olive oil in a saucepan and sauté the meatballs over medium heat.

Place garlic—unpeeled and whole or crushed and peeled—in the pan and let it sauté with the meatballs without browning. Remove the garlic and discard. Add tomato puree and let the sauce simmer for 30-60 minutes, stirring occasionally. Add water if needed. The sauce should be thick and dark red.

Polpette al limone
Meatballs with lemon, Sicily

This tastes best if the bread crumbs come from fresh bread, ideally an old country bread that is a few days old, crusts removed, which is then crushed in a food processor. Pecorino gives this dish more character than Parmesan. Sometimes pine nuts, almonds or pistachios are included in the batter as well.

3.5 oz (100 g) pecorino
1 lb (500 g) finely ground meat, either all veal or 2 parts veal
    and 1 part pork belly
3.5 oz (100 g) bread crumbs
¾ cup (1 ½ dl) chopped flat-leaf parsley
1 tsp salt
black pepper
2 eggs
zest and juice of 1 lemon
wheat flour
olive oil
1 cup (2 dl) dry white wine
hot water
8 bay leaves
1 lemon and bay leaves for garnish

Grate the pecorino and place in a bowl with the ground meat, bread crumbs, parsley, salt ground black pepper, eggs, and finely grated lemon zest. Mix everything until fully blended.

Use your hands to shape the balls so that they are about the size of golf balls. Dredge them in flour and brush away the excess. Heat some olive oil in a skillet and sauté the meatballs on medium heat until they are nicely browned on all sides.

Add wine, increase the flame, and let it simmer for a couple of minutes. Add the bay leaves and enough hot water to cover the meatballs. Let simmer until the sauce thickens. Turn the meatballs over occasionally to ensure even cooking.

Add the juice of 1 lemon and simmer for a couple of minutes more. Garnish with a bay leaf and several thin lemon slices.

Ossobuco alla Milanese
Ossobucco, Lombardy

Ossobuco means bone with a hole and refers to bone marrow, which can be absolutely delicious. If you order *ossobuco* in a restaurant in Italy you will sometimes be served special cutlery for scooping out as much of the marrow as possible. In the original Milanese recipe there are no tomatoes. You should try to make the slices of marrowbone of equal thickness so that they cook in the same amount of time. Often served with saffron risotto, *risotto alla Milanese*, or a simple risotto with Parmesan. If you wish to add tomatoes, it's entirely up to you whether you add a tablespoon of tomato puree, a peeled, seeded, and diced plum tomato, a can of whole or crushed tomatoes, or an equal amount of peeled, seeded, and diced fresh tomatoes.

4 slices veal marrowbone of about ½ lb (250 g)
salt
black pepper
flour
3 tbsp olive oil
1 yellow onion
1–2 celery stalks
1–2 carrots
3 tbsp butter
¾ cup (1 ½ dl) dry white wine
1 ½ cups (3 dl) veal stock

Gremolata:
2 tbsp chopped flat-leaf parsley
½ chopped garlic clove
1 tsp grated lemon zest (without the pith)
finely chopped anchovy fillets (optional)

Rub the meat with salt and pepper. Tie a piece of kitchen string around the marrow as though you were tying a ribbon around a gift. Dredge the marrow in flour so that it is thinly coated all around. Brown in olive oil in a large pan with a lid (you will need it later). Place the meat on a plate. Lower the flame.

Finely chop onion and carrot and dice celery. You should have an approximately equal amount of each. Melt the butter. Sauté the onion until soft; do the same for the celery, then, after a few minutes, the carrot. Return the meat to the pan. Heat the wine in a separate saucepan. Pour the wine over the meat and let it simmer until it has reduced in volume by half. Heat the stock in the saucepan. Pour half of the stock over the meat. Cover the pan and lower the flame so that the liquid is just barely simmering. Let simmer until the meat is cooked and is starting to fall off of the bone, about 1 ½–2 hours. Turn the marrow over occasionally to ensure even cooking. Add more stock if needed. It should be a well-thickened sauce.

Mix the gremolata together towards the end of the cooking time. Add to the pan and stir when the meat has finished cooking. Let it rest for a few minutes and then serve.

Ossobuco al vino rosso
Ossobucco with red wine, Piedmont

4 slices veal bone marrow, about ½ lb (250 g)
salt
black pepper
flour
3 tbsp olive oil
1 yellow onion
1–2 celery stalk
1–2 carrots
3 tbsp butter
¾ cup (1 ½ dl) dry white wine
0.8–1 lb (400-500 g) canned tomatoes, strained, crushed or whole
or the equal amount fresh, peeled, pitted and diced
1 ¼ cups (2 ½ dl) veal stock
2 tsp chopped fresh thyme or ½ tsp dried

Rub the meat with salt and pepper. Tie a piece of kitchen string around the marrow as though you were tying a ribbon around a gift. Dredge the marrow in flour so that it is thinly coated all around. Brown in olive oil in a large pan with a lid (you will need it later). Place the meat on a plate. Lower the flame.

Finely chop onion and carrot and dice celery. You should have an approximately equal amount of each. Melt the butter. Sauté the onion until soft; do the same for the celery, then, after a few minutes, the carrot. Return the meat to the pan. Pour the wine over the meat and let it simmer until it has decreased in volume by half.

Add tomatoes, stock, and spices and bring to a boil. Cover and lower the temperature so that the liquid is just barely simmering. Let simmer until the meat is cooked and is starting to fall away from the bone, about 1 ½–2 hours. Turn the veal marrow over now and then to ensure even cooking. The sauce should be quite thick. Toward the end of the cooking time, adjust the thickness of the sauce by removing the lid and letting it cook down if it is too watery, or by adding more water if it is too thick.

Ossobuchi di maiale
Pork ossobuco, Piedmont

8 slices pork marrowbone
salt
black pepper
3 tbsp olive oil
1 yellow onion
1 celery stalk
1 carrot
2 oz (60 g) pancetta
3 tbsp butter
¾ cup (1 ½ dl) dry white wine
3 tbsp tomato puree
1 ¼ cups (2 ½ dl) chicken stock

Rub the meat with salt and pepper. Tie a piece of kitchen string around the marrow as though you were tying a ribbon around a gift. Dredge the marrow in flour so that it is thinly coated all around. Brown in olive oil in a large pan with a lid (you will need it later). Place the meat on a plate. Lower the flame.

Finely chop onion, carrot, and pancetta and dice the celery. Melt the butter in the pan. Sauté the pancetta so that it releases some of its fat. Add the onion and sauté until soft; do the same for the celery, then, after a few minutes, the carrot. Heat the stock in a separate saucepan.

Add the wine to the pan and bring to a simmer. Return the meat to the pan. Add the tomato puree to the warm stock and pour the mixture into the pan. Cover and lower the temperature so that it is just barely simmering. Let simmer until the meat is cooked and is beginning to fall away from the bone, about 1 hour. Turn the marrowbone over carefully now and then to ensure even cooking. The sauce should be quite thick.

Toward the end of the cooking time, adjust the thickness of the sauce by removing the lid and letting it cook down if it is too watery, or by adding more water if it is too thick.

Stufato all'agnello, finocchio e arancia

Lamb casserole with fennel and orange, Sicily

3.5 oz (100 g) pancetta
olive oil
1 yellow onion
2 garlic cloves
2.2 lb (1 kg) ground lamb
4–6 plum tomatoes or 1 can of crushed tomatoes
2 tbsp tomato paste
¾ cup (1 ½ dl) dry white wine
1 ½ cups (3 dl) light stock
1 fennel
1 ¼ cups / 3.5 oz (2 ½ dl / 100 g) green olives, pitted
1 tsp dried oregano
salt
black pepper
zest and juice of 1 orange
parsley

Dice or shred the pancetta. Sauté in olive oil in a large pot until it releases its fat. Finely chop yellow onion and add to the pot. Crush and peel the garlic and add to the pot as well.

Increase the flame to medium–high and brown the lamb.

Blanch, peel, seed, and dice the tomatoes. (To blanch: Cut a cross in the skin at the top of the tomatoes. Place in boiling water and let them cook for a couple of minutes. Rinse with cold water. You should be able to peel them easily.)

Add the tomatoes and tomato paste to the pot. Stir and let cook for a while, 10–15 minutes. Add the wine and let everything simmer for a couple of minutes. Pour in the stock. Let everything simmer for an additional 10 minutes.

Rinse and slice the fennel (you may save the fennel fronds to use as a garnish if desired). Add the fennel to the pot with olives and dried oregano. Season with salt and freshly ground black pepper. Let it cook slowly, covered, for about 1 hour, stirring occasionally.

Scrub the orange under warm running water. Dry, grate the zest, and juice. Add the zest and juice to the pot, stirring and letting it simmer for a few minutes. Serve with chopped parsley and, if desired, the fennel fronds.

Costolette d'agnello alla calabrese
Lamb chops Calabrian style, Calabria

Bell peppers, olives, and tomatoes are generously cultivated around the toe of the Italian boot. Historically, Calabria has struggled with poverty, and this is reflected in its simple and rustic food that is characteristic of *la cucina povera*, the cuisine of the poor. These dishes succeed beautifully in bringing out all of the flavors of high-quality ingredients. This one is both easy to make and very flavorful. At the end, when the lamb chops are added to the pan, this dish becomes something of a casserole.

Use the same pan for cooking the meat and vegetables for a wonderful mingling of flavors.

8 lamb chops
salt
black pepper
1 yellow onion
6–8 plum tomatoes or 2 cans of crushed tomatoes
1 large red bell pepper

1 handful parsley
½ cup (1 dl) pitted green olives

Rub salt and freshly ground black pepper on both sides of the lamb chops. Heat 2 tablespoons of olive oil in a pan. Brown the lamb chops on both sides. Remove from pan and set aside on a plate.

Finely chop the onion and sauté over medium heat while stirring. Blanch, peel, and chop the tomatoes. Add the tomatoes to the pan and let them cook for a few minutes.

Cut open the bell pepper and remove the seeds. Chop into fairly small pieces. Place the pepper in the pan with chopped parsley and olives. Stir and season with salt and freshly ground black pepper. Lower the flame and let everything cook for 5 minutes.

Return the lamb chops to the pan; flip them once so that they pick up all of the flavors. When they are warm, remove from the pan. Serve.

Stufato di cervo
Venison stew, Trentino–Alto Adige

The northern region of Trentino–Alto Adige has more in common with Austria and Germany than with Italy, in many ways. Here you will often encounter both German and Italian names for streets and herbs. You can see the similarities in the cuisine as well, although you will also find typical southern Italian ingredients such as tomatoes and capers. This stew can also be made with other game meats, such as deer.

2.2 lbs (1 kg) venison stew meat
salt
black pepper
flour
2 tbsp olive oil
3 tbsp butter
2.5 oz (70 g) pancetta
1 yellow onion
2 celery stalk
2 carrots
1–2 garlic cloves
1 tbsp rosemary
1 handful fresh sage
1 handful leaf parsley
1 ¼ cups (2 ½ dl) dry white wine
2–3 plum tomatoes or ½ can crushed tomatoes
3 spice carnations
1 tbsp capers
2 cups (5 dl) beef or other meat stock

Dry the stew pieces and season with salt and freshly ground black pepper. Dredge in flour. Brush any excess flour away. Heat the olive oil in a medium pot. Melt the butter. Brown the stew pieces in two rounds until they have a nice color all around. Place on a plate.

Sauté shredded or diced pancetta until it releases its fat. Finely chop the onion, celery, and carrot. You should have roughly the same amount of each. Add the onion and sauté until soft, stirring attentively.

Add ingredients in the following order, sautéing each until soft before adding the next one: celery, carrots, then crushed and peeled garlic. Chop rosemary, sage, and parsley and stir in with the other ingredients. Sauté for a few minutes. Pour the wine into the pan and let simmer for a few minutes more.

Scald, peel, seed, and dice the tomatoes. Return the meat to the pot. Add tomatoes, spice carnations, capers, and stock. Bring to a boil and then reduce the heat and let simmer, covered, for about 2 hours, stirring ocasionally. Add more water if needed. Top it off with chopped parsley before serving.

Cinghiale alla viterbese
Viterbo-style wild boar, Lazio

Viterbo is situated 50 miles north of Rome and was built about one thousand years ago, although the Etruscans already had a city there at the time. Wild boar is very popular in Italy, both as a cured meat and in stews and sauces. You can find wild boar dishes all over the country, from Tuscany to Lazio to the deep South.

1.5 lbs (800 g) wild boar stew meat
1 bottle red wine
2 rosemary sprigs
1 tbsp fresh marjoram leaves
2 garlic cloves
1 small yellow onion
olive oil
salt
black pepper
14 oz (400 g) plum tomatoes or 1 can crushed
1 small dried peperoncino, crushed

Rinse the meat in cold water. Place in a stainless steel or glass bowl. Heat wine, 1 rosemary sprig, marjoram leaves, 1 garlic clove, and peeled and quartered onion in a saucepan. Let cool, pour over the meat, cover with plastic wrap, and let marinate in the fridge overnight.

Remove the meat from the marinade; set the marinade aside. Finely chop 1 garlic clove and the rest of the rosemary. Heat some olive oil in a pan and sauté garlic and rosemary until the garlic is just starting to brown. Season the boar meat with salt and black pepper and brown it in the pan. Add some of the marinade to the pan and bring to a simmer.

Blanch, peel, seed, and dice the tomatoes. Mix tomatoes and peperoncino in with the ingredients in the pan. Let it simmer under a lid until the meat is cooked, about 45 minutes. Add water if needed.

Pollo alla 'ncip 'ncap
Chicken with lots of garlic, Marche

The name of this dish may be onomatopoeic, in that it sounds a little like chopping a chicken into pieces. It is also called *pollo all'arrabiata*—a name that refers to the spiciness of the peperoncini, as with the similarly named penne dish—or simply *pollo in padella*, chicken in a skillet.

1 fresh whole chicken
salt
black pepper
olive oil
½ cup (1 dl) dry white wine
1 rosemary sprig
1 handful of sage leaves
10–15 garlic cloves, with peel
1–2 small dried peperoncini, depending on potency, crushed
4–6 plum tomatoes

Cut the chicken into 8 pieces (2 thighs, 2 drumsticks, and halve the breasts to create the other 4 pieces). Season with salt and freshly ground black pepper.

Heat olive oil in a pan. Brown the chicken pieces until golden over medium heat. Pour the wine in the pan, increase the flame, and bring to a simmer. Add rosemary, sage, unpeeled garlic cloves, and peperoncino. Reduce flame to low, cover the pan, and let simmer for 20–30 minutes, until the chicken is cooked and falling away from the bone. Remove the seeds of the tomatoes, cut in large pieces, and let them cook with the chicken briefly. Serve.

Pollo in umido al limone
Chicken in lemon sauce, Campania

1 yellow onion
3 celery stalks
3 carrots
olive oil
3 garlic cloves
a few rosemary sprigs
5 bay leaves
2 lemons
1 fresh whole chicken
salt
black pepper
flour
sunflower oil or canola oil
½ cup (1 dl) dry white wine
2 ½ cups (5 dl) water

Finely chop yellow onion, celery, and carrots. Heat olive oil in a pan. Sauté the onion until soft. Do the same with the celery, then, after a few minutes, the carrots. Crush and peel the garlic cloves and let them sauté with the rest. Add rosemary, bay leaves, and a large piece of lemon peel without the pith.

While the vegetables are cooking: Cut the chicken into 8 pieces (2 thighs, 2 drumsticks, and halve the breasts for the other 4 pieces). Season with salt and freshly ground black pepper. Dredge in flour so that they are evenly coated. Shake off any excess flour.

Heat sunflower oil or canola oil in a separate pan. Brown the chicken until golden on high heat.

Move the chicken into the vegetable pan. Halve the lemons and squeeze the juice over the chicken. Add wine, increase the flame, and bring to a boil. Add water, bring to a boil, then lower the temperature again. Cover, leaving the lid slightly ajar, and simmer for about 1 hour. Let the sauce cook down and thicken well.

Pollo alla romana
Roman-style chicken, Lazio

This is usually served at Italian trattorias with some bread, which is used to pick up the delicious sauce. Sometimes it is made with both red and green bell peppers. Red peppers make the dish sweeter whereas the green peppers make it more bitter. Using green bell peppers exclusively is more authentically Roman.

If you wish, you can also give the dish some character by adding pancetta.

2 garlic cloves
olive oil
2 oz (60 g) pancetta or bacon (optional)
1 chicken
salt
black pepper
½ –¾ cup (1 ½ dl) dry white wine
3 green bell peppers
1 lb (500 g) tomato puree

Crush and peel the garlic. Sauté in olive oil until it has browned slightly. If using pancetta, first let it sauté in olive oil until it releases its fat, then add and sauté the garlic. Remove the garlic from the pan and save.

Cut the chicken into pieces that are approximately equal in size. Season with salt and freshly ground black pepper. Brown the chicken pieces in the fat. Pour the wine in the pan and let simmer for 5 minutes.

Remove the seeds from the bell peppers and cut into strips. Add bell peppers, garlic, and tomato puree to the pan. Let simmer, covered, for about 30 minutes. The chicken is ready when the meat is falling away from the bone and the drippings are clear. The stew will come out best if it is allowed to cook slowly. Add water if needed. Season with salt and black pepper.

Pollo alla cacciatora
The hunter's wife's chicken, Tuscany

There are many varieties of *Pollo alla cacciatora*. In Emilia–Romagna, the dish includes yellow or green bell peppers, in Piedmont they use carrot or celery, Sicilians make it with capers and red wine vinegar, in Friuli–Venice Giuila they add mushrooms, and Abruzzo's version includes pork belly, garlic, sage, and rosemary. The recipe below hails from Tuscany and uses garlic and peperoncino. Chicken used to be less common in Italy and was mostly only served on special occasions, for instance, a filling meal before the hunt. Perhaps that is how it got its name.

1 large yellow onion
1 garlic clove
1 carrot
1 celery stalk
olive oil
1 small dried peperoncino, crushed
1 large fresh chicken
salt
black pepper
¾ cup (1 ½ dl) dry white wine
6 plum tomatoes or 1 can whole, crushed, or pureed tomatoes
flat-leaf parsley

Finely chop onion, carrot, and celery. Sauté until soft in olive oil. Let the peperoncino sauté with the onion.

Sauté the onion until soft without browning. Add and sauté celery. Add the carrot and sauté. Place everything on a plate.

Cut the chicken into smaller, stew-sized pieces. Season with salt and freshly ground black pepper and brown in olive oil until golden. Add the wine and bring to a simmer.

Blanch, deseed, and dice the tomatoes (if using canned tomatoes, just dice them). Add to the pan with the sautéed vegetables. Let simmer under a lid for about 30 minutes.

The chicken is ready when it is falling away from the bones and the drippings are clear. The stew tastes better if it is allowed to cook slowly. Add more water if needed. Top off with chopped parsley and serve.

You may also let black olives boil with the stew for added flavor, or you can sauté anchovies with the onion at the beginning.

119

PESCE *fish & shellfish*

Fish is served as a *secondo piatto* or *secondo* and is usually accompanied by a vegetable side, or *contorno*.

No matter where you are in Italy you are almost always near the sea. Out of twenty regions, only four—Piedmont, Lombardy, Trentino–Alto Adige, and Umbria—have no coastline. But even in these regions, there are rivers and lakes with a lot of fish. Fish and shellfish are a vital part of Italian cuisine.

Fish is a seasonal ingredient; it is caught and eaten the time of year that it's at its best. Fresh fish is always best, of course. In fact, there is a law that states that if frozen fish is used at a restaurant, it has to be indicated on the menu.

Preserved fish also has a place in Italian cooking. It is impossible to imagine Italian cuisine without anchovies, which may be called both *acciughe* and *alici*. At *supermercati*, you will find a large selection and at the fish markets they are sold in barrels. Certain dishes should not be made with fresh tuna, but rather with canned, which there is a large selection of in Italy.

Pesce spada alla stemperata
Sweet and sour swordfish with potatoes, Sicily

Sweet, sour, and salty flavors are very popular in Sicily, an aspect of its culinary heritage that dates back to its Arabic, Moorish past. *Stemperare* means to dilute or to take the life out of something. In this case, it refers to how the vinegar cooks off during cooking.
You may also make just the sauce, without the potatoes, to accompany swordfish or tuna.

1 lb (500 g) firm potatoes
2 large yellow onion
olive oil
1 small dried peperoncino, crushed
2 celery stalks
15 green olives, pitted
2 large firm potatoes
2 tbsp capers
4 tsp sugar
4 tbsp red wine vinegar
4 swordfish steaks
salt
black pepper
flour
flat-leaf parsley

Preheat the oven to 400 F (200 C). Peel the potatoes and cut into slices about 1 inch (1 ½ cm) thick. Boil in salted water.

Finely chop the onion and sauté until soft in olive oil. Let the peperoncino sauté as well. Slice the celery. Chop the olives. Blanch, peel, seed, and dice the tomatoes.

Let the olives and celery sauté for a couple of minutes. Add the tomatoes and sauté briefly as well.

Add capers, sugar, and vinegar.

Increase the flame and let the vinegar quickly cook off, stirring constantly. The celery should still be a little firm. Season. There should be a balance between the sweet and the sour. Adjust if needed. Remove from the stove.

Dry the swordfish. Season with salt and freshly ground black pepper. Dredge in flour. Heat some olive oil in a pan and fry until golden over medium heat.

Grease a baking dish. Cover the bottom of the pan with potato slices. Place the fish on top and cover with the sauce.

Bake in the oven for about 10 minutes. Top it off with chopped parsley before serving.

Tonno alla griglia con salmoriglio
Grilled tuna with salmoriglio sauce, Calabria, Sicily

Grilled tuna and swordfish make up some of the most common restaurant dishes along the coast, especially in southern Italy. Salmoriglio sauce works partly as a marinade and later as a sauce for the grilled fish. Whole anchovies—or herring—can also be brushed with the sauce and grilled. The same goes for lobster and shrimp. Salmoriglio is also great with grilled lamb.

2 lemons
The juice and zest if 1 lemon
¾ cup (1 ½ dl) olive oil
1 small chopped fresh red chili or 1 small dried peperoncino, crushed
1 garlic clove
6 tbsp chopped flat-leaf parsley
2 tbsp fresh oregano or 2 tbsp dried
salt
black pepper
4 tuna steaks
lemon wedges

Grate the zest of 1 lemon, taking care to avoid the pith. Blend with lemon juice, olive oil, peperoncino or fresh chili, finely chopped garlic, parsley, and oregano. Season with salt and freshly ground black pepper.

Brush the sauce on the fish and let it marinate for about 30 minutes. Don't allow it to marinate it for any longer, as the acidity cooks the fish. Save the leftover sauce for serving.

Grill the fish on a grill or on a stovetop griddle. Serve with lemon wedges.

Sogliola alla fiorentina
Sole on spinach bed, Tuscany

Spinach is especially popular in Florence and is often used as a bed for various dishes. *Alla fiorentina*—Florence style—will often be used to mean just that.

8 fillets of sole or another flat fish or white fish
salt
black pepper
juice of ½ lemon
2 lb (1 kg) fresh spinach or 1 lb (500 g) frozen whole spinach
2 tbsp butter
freshly grated nutmeg
1 small yellow onion
3 tbsp (50 g) butter
½ tsp dried thyme
1 cup (2 dl) dry white wine
2 oz (50 g) wheat flour
2 ½ cups (5 dl) milk
2 oz (50 g) Parmesan

Preheat the oven to 450 F (225 C).

Season the fish with salt and freshly ground black pepper. Drizzle with lemon juice.

Fresh spinach: Rinse and wash the spinach. Empty in a large saucepan, add a pinch of salt, and let it cook, covered, without added water. Stir occasionally. Remove from the stove when the leaves have condensed. Let the spinach drain in a strainer.

Frozen spinach: Thaw the spinach. Squeeze the excess liquid out and separate the leaves. Sauté the spinach lightly in butter for a few minutes. Season with salt and pepper.

Grate nutmeg on top of the spinach and stir.

Make the *besciamella:* Finely chop onions and sauté until soft in a pan in the 3 tablespoons butter. Add the thyme let the contents of the pan sauté together for a bit. Add the wine, increase the heat, and let simmer until the wine has almost completely evaporated. Add the flour and stir until there are no lumps. Add some milk and whisk lightly. Add the rest of the milk a little at a time while whisking.

Let the sauce come to a boil, simmer while stirring for about 5 minutes. Season with salt and freshly ground black pepper. Spice with a pinch of grated nutmeg.

Grease a baking dish with butter. Cover the bottom with spinach. On top of this, place a layer of fish fillets. Cover everything with the sauce. Grate Parmesan and sprinkle on top. Bake in the oven until the cheese is light golden brown, about 10–15 minutes.

Pesce spada menta
Swordfish with mint, Calabria

4 swordfish steaks
2 garlic cloves
salt
dry, day-old country bread
olive oil
2 tbsp white wine vinegar
1 handful mint leaves

Peel and halve the garlic cloves. Rub the fish with the garlic and then with salt.

Grate the bread to make fresh bread crumbs, or tear and place in a food processor. Pat the bread crumbs into the fish.

Heat olive oil in a skillet over medium heat and fry the fish until it is light golden brown. Let it drain on a paper towel.

Arrange the fish on a serving plate. Drizzle vinegar on top. Finely chop mint and add on top of the fish. Let sit for about 30 minutes before serving.

Coda di rospo piccata

Monkfish with capers and lemon, Lazio

Piccata usually refers to a slice of veal that has been pounded thin and fried in butter with lemon, capers, and parsley. Here we use monkfish instead. The monkfish flesh is not that different from veal, because both are light and firm. Many even call monkfish "the veal of the sea."

1.5 lbs (750 g) monkfish fillet
¾ cup (1 ½ dl) flour
salt
black pepper
2 tbsp olive oil
3 tbsp butter
¾ cup (1 ½ dl) dry white wine
3 tbsp lemon juice
2 tbsp capers
flat-leaf parsley
lemon

Carefully cut and remove the gray membrane from the monkfish using a very sharp knife. (The membrane does not taste good and makes the monkfish flesh contract when cooked.) Cut slices that are about 1 cm / 1/3 inch thick on a slant, the same way you would cut salmon, so that the surface of the pieces turn out a tad bit larger.

Carefully pound each piece under the protection of plastic wrap or parchment paper. They should be about 5 mm thick when you are done.

Pour the flour into a deep plate. Add salt and freshly ground black pepper and mix. Dredge the fish in the flour. Place on a plate and dry.

Heat olive oil in a pan, then add the butter and let it melt. Fry a few slices of fish at a time on medium heat. They are ready when they are a light golden brown.

Arrange the fish on a warm plate and cover with foil. Add wine, lemon juice, and capers to the pan, increase the flame, and let simmer until the sauce has thickened a little.

Add the chopped parsley. Pour the sauce over the fish and serve right away. Green asparagus or lightly boiled broccoli work well as sides to this dish.

Finely chop the onion. Heat a few tablespoons of olive oil in a pan and sauté the onion until soft. Rinse the anchovies, dry, and finely chop. Decrease the flame and carefully sauté the anchovies until they melt and dissolve.

Add peperoncino, capers, chopped parsley, and bread crumbs. Sauté, stirring so that all of the flavors blend together. Add more olive oil if needed.

Pour the mussel broth over the mussels in the baking dish. Cover with the bread crumbs. Drizzle olive oil on top and drizzle with lemon juice. Place in the oven and cook until the bread crumbs are golden brown.

Serve right away with good bread for soaking up all of the delicious juices.

Cozze ripiene
Mussels au gratin, Sicily

3.3 lbs (1 ½ kg) mussels with shells
¾ cup (1 ½ dl) dry white wine
2 garlic cloves
1 small yellow onion
olive oil
6 anchovy fillets
1 small dried peperoncino, crushed
3 tbsp (50 g) capers
1 handful flat-leaf parsley
1 ½ cups (3 dl) bread crumbs
juice of 1 lemon

Preheat the oven to 440 F (225 C).

Scrub the mussels. Discard any that are broken or don't close when you tap them against a hard surface, like the countertop.

Place the mussels, wine, and crushed garlic cloves in a large pot, cover, and cook on high heat until the mussels open. Remove and discard any that have remained closed. Drain the broth from the pot and save. Remove the half of the shell that the meat is not fastened to and discard. Place the other mussels in a large baking dish in one layer with the meat facing upwards.

Cacciucco alla livornese
Livorno-style fish soup, Tuscany

This is more of a stew than a soup. Soups similar to this are made all over the Italian coast. Both Livorno and Viareggio, two cities on the Tuscan coast, claim ownership of this dish. *Cacciucco alla viareggina* is sometimes served with a rock in the bottom of the bowl, which is another way of referring to the fact that originally this dish was made with everything caught in the fisherman's net.

1 yellow or red onion
4 tbsp olive oil
2 garlic cloves
1 small dried peperoncino, crushed
1 handful chopped parsley
1 celery stalk
1 tbsp tomato puree
1 cup (2 dl) red wine
14 oz (400 g) preserved cherry tomatoes
2 ½ cups (5 dl) fish stock
14 oz (400 g) white fish
14 oz (400 g) squid, shrimp, and mussels
salt
black pepper
country bread

Finely chop the onion and sauté until soft in olive oil. Crush the garlic clove and let it sauté with

the peperoncino and half of the chopped parsley. Finely chop the celery and sauté until soft.

Add tomato puree and sauté, stirring, until it darkens and becomes sweet. Add the wine and bring to a simmer. Stir in the tomatoes, return it to a simmer, and let it continue for about 30 minutes. Dilute with fish stock.

Cut the fish into smaller, stew-sized pieces. Season with salt and freshly ground black pepper.

If using fresh mussels: Scrub and rinse the mussels, throw out the ones with broken shells and the ones that don't close when you tap them again a hard surface.

Place the mussels in a large pot and cook on high heat, covered, until the mussels open. Discard any that have not opened. Remove the broth from the pot and add to the soup.

There are two ways to cook the fish, shellfish, and squid. One option is to place them in the soup, the larger pieces first, and let them simmer very slowly. As an alternative, you can steam or let them simmer in as little water as possible in a separate saucepan. This method allows you to keep the whiteness of the fish, which contrasts beautifully with the red soup.

Add the broth to the soup. Small squid and cut pieces of fish cook quickly. If they cook for too long, they become rubbery. Add fresh boiled shrimp at the end. Season with salt and freshly ground black pepper.

Sprinkle the rest of the parsley on top and serve with toasted country bread that has been rubbed with garlic, or place the bread at the bottom of a plate and pour the soup on top.

Stefano Catenacci

EVERY SUNDAY THE FAMILY GATHERS in his parents' house to eat dinner.

"A real Sunday dinner with *antipasto, primo, secondo*, and *dolci*," says Stefano Catenacci. 20 people in their little three-bedroom apartment. "We're Italian; we live to eat. And afterwards we watch Italian soccer on TV."

Papà Vincenzo is from Rome and Mamma Matilde is originally from Naples but grew up in Rome. So Stefano's roots place him smack in the middle of Rome, even if he was born in Sweden.

"My mother and father have always said that inside the walls of our home we're in Italy. It was important to them that we spoke Italian, which I am very grateful for today."

The original plan was that Papà Vincenzo would open a restaurant in Holland with a very close friend of his, but both the friend and the money disappeared. Vincenzo was too embarrassed to return to Italy, so instead he moved to Sweden.

STEFANO'S FIRST JOB WAS as a twelve-year-old at the family restaurant Cainia at Söder in Stockholm during the 1970s.

"Only my father, my mom, and I worked the kitchen. Any other way was simply never an option. Not for my big brother Alessandro either." In 1987, he took over the club empire Wretman, which among others includes Operakällaren. Sandro takes care of

the business end of things and Stefano takes care of the food.

"But on Sundays my father cooks," Stefano tells us. "My father's food is good enough for my mother. Give her anything else and she complains."

Stefano eats freely from all regions of Italy, whereas mamma and papa prefer the cuisines of Rome and Naples. And sometimes Tuscany.

The family has always kept up with Italy and goes back at least once a year.

"I miss the chaos of Italy when I'm in Sweden. When I'm in Italy, I miss Sweden's order."

When Stefano was growing up, there was really no legitimate Italian food to be found in Sweden. Today, both the supply and the knowledge of Italian cuisine have improved. The Carenacci brothers' new restaurant in Stockholm still has ties to their roots. It is called Caina.

"Here we really get to cook with out hearts. We make the food we grew up with."

Merluzzo con caponatina
Back of cod with vegetable compote

This dish is commonly served at our new Caina at Norrmalmstorg. Inspired by Southern Italy with a small *caponata* and a thin slice of *bottarga* and a smooth pesto sauce. Stefano uses *bottarga di muggine*, grey mullet. There is also *bottarga di tonno*.

4 portion-sized pieces of back of cod with the skin.
Olive oil

Caponatina:
1 zucchini
1 eggplant
1 red bell pepper
olive oil
1 small handful   *of*
pine nuts

pesto sauce or basil
sauce:
pesto or basil
olive oil

Set the oven to 390 F (200 C). Fry the cod with the skin facing down in a very hot pan with olive oil until they are nicely brown with a crispy surface. Place the fish with the skin facing upwards in an oven pan. Stick a thermometer into the middle of one of the pieces of fish. Cook in the oven until the thermometer shows 90 F (34 C).

Finely dice zucchini, eggplant, and bell pepper. Brown quickly in olive oil on high heat with the pine nuts. The vegetables should be browned nicely but still maintain some chewing resistance.

Make the pesto sauce in a food processor. Stir in additional olive oil and pass through a thread sieve. You can also make a basil oil: mix a generous amount of basil and olive oil and pass through a sieve.

Slice the *bottarga* lengthwise and brush it shiny with olive oil.

Arrange on a plate with salad.

Sarde ripiene alla siciliana
Stuffed anchovies with fennel, Sicily

Herring or Baltic herring is a great replacement for the anchovies in this recipe. In Sicily they also make *sarde a beccafico* where you tie the fish fillets together with the filling in between, dip in egg and bread crumbs, and later fry in olive oil. The name stems from a bird that likes fennel. The filling can vary, but it can contain, for instance, anchovies, olives, raisins, pine nuts, parsley, and almonds.

14 oz (400 g) herring or Baltic herring
1 yellow onion
1 fennel
3-4 tbsp olive oil
0.8 oz (25 g) pine nuts
1 garlic clove
½ cup (1 dl) bread crumbs+ 1 tbsp
1 handful leaf parsley
salt
black pepper
1 lemon + juice

Warm the oven to 390 F (200 C). Rinse and dry the fish. Slice the onion thinly. Slice the fennel thinly. Cut the hard stem in the middle away.

Heat olive oil in a pan. Sauté onion and fennel until soft without browning. Sprinkle a pinch of salt on top to make this easier. Let the pine nuts and the garlic clove (crushed and peeled or whole with the skin still on) sauté with the fish after a while. Remove the garlic when it starts to brown. Add the bread crumbs and brown. Chop the leaf parsley. Set aside about 1 tbsp of bread crumbs and parsley. Add the rest to the pan. Season with salt and ground black pepper. Remove from the stove.

Grease an oven pan with olive oil. Place half of the fish fillets with the skin facing down. Season with salt and pepper. Spread the filling out on top of the fish. Place the remaining fish fillets on top. Add salt and pepper. Blend the remaining parsley and bread crumbs and sprinkle on top of the fish. Squeeze some lemon juice and drizzle olive oil on top. Bake in the oven until the fish is cooked and the dish is golden, about 10 minutes. Serve right away with lemon wedges, or eat cooled.

Sarde ripiene alla pugliese
Stuffed anchovies with pecorino, Puglia

Herring may replace anchovies. If you are able to find whole herring instead of fillets, it is even more similar to the original dish. In that case, place the filling on top of the fish.

14 oz (400 g) herring or Baltic herring
2 eggs
1.7 oz (50 g) pecorino
½ cup (1 dl) bread crumbs
leaf parsley
olive oil
salt
black pepper

Set the oven to 390 F (200 C). Rinse and dry the fish. Stir eggs, freshly grated pecorino, bread crumbs, a few tablespoons of chopped parsley, and olive oil into a blend that holds together but is not too compact.

Grease a baking pan with olive oil. Place the fish fillets with the skin facing downwards. Season with salt and freshly ground pepper. Cover with the filling and place the rest of the fish fillets on top. Add salt and pepper. If you are preparing it with the filling on top, you can sprinkle that on top of the fish. Drizzle some olive oil over the fish. Bake in the oven until the fish is cooked, about 10 minutes.

Pesce in saor
Preserved fish, Veneto

Saor means flavor in the Venetian dialect. This is an old-fashioned way of preserving fish, basically pickling. *Sarde in saor* is most common these days and is often served as *cichetti*, the Venetian bars' mouthfuls that are eaten like Spanish tapas. In previous times, poor people made *pesce in saor* with anchovies, the middle class would use a nicer fish, and the upper class would make it with sole.

The spices may vary, but they are all reminiscent of the Venetian close ties with the East and the trade of exotic spices like spice carnations and coriander. This recipe has Arabic influences and is similar to the flavors of Sicily.

1 lb (500 g) herring, Baltic herring, or flat fish
1 lb (500 g) yellow onion
olive oil
salt

1 ¼ cups (2 ½ dl) dry white wine
½ cup (1 dl) white wine vinegar
3 tbsp (50 g) pine nuts
3 tbsp (50 g) raisins
3 tbsp (50 g) sugar
2 bay leaves
black pepper
flour

Slice the onion thinly and sauté until soft without browning in olive oil. Add a pinch of salt to make this easier. You may also add a little water if it gets too dry. Add wine, white wine vinegar, pine nuts, raisins, sugar, and bay leaves. Season with salt and ground black pepper. Let it boil for about 15 minutes.

Rinse and dry the fish. Salt and pepper lightly. Turn fish in flour. Remove any surplus flour. Fry in olive oil on high heat until it obtains a nice color on both sides. Let it drain on a paper towel.

Place a layer of the onion blend in the bottom of a serving plate or a low dish. Arrange the fish on top and cover with the rest of the blend. Let it cool, cover with plastic wrap, and let it sit in the fridge for at least 24 hours. Serve cold.

CONTORNI E VERDURE *sides & vegetables*

The Italian relationship to vegetables is nothing short of love. Fresh, local, and in season, vegetables are often prepared under the principle of never doing more than what is absolutely necessary to lift the flavors.

It is not uncommon to serve multiple vegetable dishes with a meal. First as *antipasto*, later as a part of *primo*, and then as *contorni*, sides to *secondo* with meat, fowl, and fish.

Many meals in Italy can be fully vegetarian, even if the term itself is not used as commonly there. It is also common that the dish is vegetarian with the exception of one ingredient that is mostly added for flavoring, for instance pancetta or pork belly.

Mixed green salad, *insulate mist*, is served as is with sea salt and olive oil. Richer salads are not as common, as they preferably serve each vegetable separately.

Some dishes in this chapter may be served as *antipasto*.

Cavolo rosso
Red cabbage with pork belly and wine, Trentino–Alto Adige

1 small head of red cabbage
1.7 oz (50 g) salted pork belly
2 tbsp butter
1 yellow onion
salt
black pepper
a couple pinches of sugar
1 cup (2 dl) red wine

Remove the outer leaves of the cabbage. Cut the head in four wedges and remove the hard stem in the middle. Cut into thin shreds.

Dice the meat. Brown in butter. Remove from the pan and move onto a plate.

Finely chop the onion and sauté until soft without browning. Stir in the cabbage. Season with salt and freshly ground black pepper and sprinkle the sugar on top.

Pour the wine in the pan and let it simmer under a lid for about 30 minutes. Sprinkle the meat on top and serve.

Piselli alla pancetta
Green peas with pancetta, Lazio

Our frozen peas are perfect. Fresher peas are hard to find since ours are frozen only hours after harvesting. This is a simple and quick side that goes with most dishes, meat, fish, or fowl. Instead of pancetta, you may also use air-dried ham, for instance Parma. With some toasted bread, this is a great little snack for when you want something in the evening.

½ lb (300 g) peas
3.5 oz (100 g) smoked pancetta
3 tbsp butter

Let the frozen peas thaw a little. Cut the pancetta in fine shreds and brown carefully on low heat in butter. Add the peas, stirring until they are warm all the way through. Serve right away.

Piselli alla menta
Green peas with mint, Veneto

Piselli is the Italian name for peas, but in Vento they are really called *bisi*. At the end of May and beginning of June there are multiple *Festa dei bisi* and *segra dei bisi* in Veneto. This recipe may also be varied with basil and leaf parsley instead of mint.

½ lb (300 g) peas
1 small yellow onion
3 tbsp butter
¼ cup (½ dl) water
½ tsp salt
fresh mint

Let frozen peas thaw somewhat.

Finely chop the onion and sauté in a saucepan until soft without browning. Add peas, water, and salt and simmer under a lid until the peas are soft. Remove the saucepan from the stove.

Chop a generous amount of mint, blend with the peas, and serve.

Insalata di barbabietole con menta
Red beet salad with mint

Reed beets and/or yellow beets
Fresh mint

Dressing:
4 tbsp olive oil
1 tbsp white wine vinegar
salt
black pepper

Boil the beets until almost soft under a lid. Drain and let them cool in cold water.
Pull the skin off and cut into smaller pieces. Place beets in a bowl with the mint leaves. Blend the dressing, pour on top, and toss.

Melanzane grigliate
Grilled preserved eggplant, Sicily

You may also make this recipe with zucchini.

2 eggplants
2 garlic cloves
½ cup (1 dl) olive oil
juice of 1 lemon or 3 tbsp white wine vinegar
1 small dried peperoncino
salt
black pepper
fresh basil or dried oregano
leaf parsley

Slice the eggplant thinly. Grill on a hot grill pan or brush with a little olive oil and grill in the oven or on the grill.

Peel and slice the garlic cloves. Blend a marinade with olive oil, juice from 1 lemon or white wine vinegar, garlic slices, peperoncino, salt, and freshly ground black pepper.

Place the eggplant slices in the marinade. Flavor with grated fresh basil or dried oregano and chopped leaf parsley. Keep in the fridge.

Carote in agrodolce
Sweet and sour carrots

8 carrots
1 tbsp butter
3 tbsp white wine vinegar
2 tbsp sugar
salt

Peel the carrots and slice in about ¼-inch thick slices.

Melt the butter in a saucepan. Add vinegar and sugar and stir until the sugar is dissolved.

Add the carrots and salt and stir. Let it simmer under a lid until the carrots are cooked, not completely soft, but still with some resistance.

Season with salt. Serve warm or cold.

Peperoni arrostiti
Roasted preserved bell peppers, Basilicata

4 large bell peppers, red, yellow, or orange
2 garlic cloves
½ cup (1 dl) olive oil
juice of 1 lemon or 3 tbsp white wine vinegar
salt
black pepper
fresh basil
leaf parsley

Roast the bell peppers on a grill or directly over a gas burner. You can also cut them in half, place them with the skin pointing upwards on a baking sheet, and roast them in the oven at the highest temperature. The bell peppers should be completely black.

Let them cool and then pull the skin off. Do not rinse them in water, as the flavors will wash away.

Cut open the peppers and remove the cores. Slice in elongated pieces.

Peel and slice the garlic cloves. Blend a marinade with olive oil, lemon juice or white wine vinegar, garlic slices, salt, and fresh ground black pepper.

Place the bell peppers in the marinade. Flavor with fresh basil and chopped leaf parsley. Keep in the fridge.

Grigliata di vegetali
Grilled vegetables

Grilled vegetables are a suitable *contorni* for almost anything or can be served as *antipasto*. Marinate and grill outside on a coal grill or inside in a grill pan.

2 zucchinis
1 eggplant
1 yellow bell pepper
1 red bell pepper
4 firm tomatoes

Marinade:
5 tbsp olive oil
2 tbsp white wine vinegar
2 tbsp chopped fresh basil
2 tbsp chopped fresh mint
salt
black pepper

Blend the marinade. Make sure that the coal grill or grill pan is very hot.

Slice the zucchinis and eggplant lengthwise very thinly. Remove the cores of the bell peppers and cut them in wide shreds. Cut the tomatoes in half.

Dip vegetables in the marinade and place them on the grill. Grill them in two rounds. Be patient: don't be too quick with turning them because the vegetables will stick. If they are allowed the time to form black grill patterns, they won't stick. Turn and brush marinade on the other side.

Grill the tomatoes last as they release a lot of fluids. Brush marinade on the cut surface and place the tomatoes with the cut side facing downwards.

Melanzane marinate
Marinated eggplant, Calabria

1.3 lbs (600 g) eggplant
salt
⅔ cup (1 ¾ dl) olive oil
3 garlic cloves
10 fresh mint leaves
1 small fresh red chili pepper or 1 small dried peperoncino
1 tbsp capers (optional)

Slice the eggplant in slices about ¼-inch thick, lengthwise or across. Sprinkle salt on top and place in a sieve under pressure—cover with a plate and set a bowl or saucepan filled with water on top. Let it drain for at least 30 minutes. Remove the salt with water and dry.

Heat a frying pan. Brush the eggplant slices with some oil. Brown until golden on high heat.

Chop the garlic and mint leaves (and fresh chili if this is what you are using). Rinse and chop the capers. Blend garlic, mint, peperoncino/chili, and capers. Season with salt and ground black pepper.

Place a layer of fried eggplant slices in a baking pan. Sprinkle the spice blend on top. Continue with another layer and then the spice blend. Pour the remaining olive oil on top. Let it marinate in the fridge overnight or for at least 6 hours.

Melanzane marinate
Marinated eggplant, Emilia-Romagna

1.3 lbs (600 g) eggplant
salt
olive oil
1 handful leaf parsley
1 handful basil leaves
1 handful sage leaves
3 garlic cloves
salt
black pepper
⅓ cup (¾ dl) white wine or red wine vinegar

Prepare the eggplant slices as the recipe above, drain, and fry.

Chop leaf parsley, basil, and sage. Finely chop the garlic cloves. Blend herbs and garlic. Season with salt and ground black pepper.

Place a layer of fried eggplant slices in a baking pan. Sprinkle the spice blend on top. Add a few drops of vinegar. Continue with a second layer of eggplant, spice blend, and vinegar. Let it marinate in the fridge overnight or for at least 6 hours.

Insalata de couscous al limone
Couscous salad with lemon, Sicily

1 ½ cup (3 dl) couscous
chicken bouillon
1 lemon, zest and juice
3 tbsp fresh sage or leaf parsley
3 tbsp olive oil
1 ½ tbsp capers
3 tbsp (about 1 oz (30 g)) pine nuts

Prepare the couscous with chicken bouillon by following the directions on the package. Toss the couscous with a fork.

Grate the zest from the lemon while avoiding the bitter white part. Squeeze the juice.

Chop the sage leaves or leaf parsley.

Heat half of the olive oil in a skillet. Brown capers, lemon zest, sage or parsley, and pine nuts while stirring until the pine nuts have gained some color.

Add the couscous with the lemon juice and the rest of the oil. Serve at room temperature.

Funghi sott'olio
Mushrooms in oil, Calabria

Mushrooms in oil are popular all over Italy. It tastes great with cured meats. Toward the south, they spice with peperoncino. The Italians are dedicated mushroom pickers. Cars can suddenly, and quite dangerously, stop and park to pick mushrooms.

mushrooms
2 parts water
1 part white wine vinegar
salt
garlic cloves
herbs: rosemary, thyme, oregano or bay leaf
peperoncino if wanted
olive oil or both olive oil and sunflower oil

Rinse and wash the mushrooms. Let them simmer in water, white wine vinegar, and salt to taste for 10-15 minutes.

Drain in a sieve. Dry the mushrooms with a paper towel.

Place in a glass jar with a few peeled and sliced garlic

cloves, herbs, and peperoncino to taste. Pour olive oil or both olive oil and sunflower oil on top until the mushrooms are covered.

Feel free to let them sit for a few days to let the flavors develop.

Funghi alla diavola
Hot mushroom in red wine, Tuscany

Use your own mushrooms or buy, for instance, regular champignons and brown champignons.

1.3 lbs (600 g) mushroom
2 garlic cloves
4 tbsp olive oil
1-2 small dried peperoncinos, crushed
1 large yellow onion
¾ cup (1 ½ dl) red wine
salt
black pepper

Rinse and wash the mushrooms. Dry them off.

Crush and peel the garlic cloves. Heat olive oil in a pan and sauté the garlic until soft for a few minutes without browning it.

Slice the onion thinly and let it sauté while stirring until soft without browning. Add the mushrooms and sauté until they release liquid and are starting to brown.

Add the wine to the pan and boil for about 20 minutes. Stir now and then. The wine should almost boil away completely. Season with salt and fresh ground pepper.

Francesca Wassenius

"THE KITCHEN IS MY REGNO, MY KINGDOM."

After more than twenty years in Sweden, her language is still sprinkled with Italian words, and Francesca Wassenius is most definitely Italian. Or Sicilian.

She was born near the center of the island in Caltanissetta, a city with roots from the 400s before Christ, and the place where the liqueur Amaro Averna is produced.

"Once a Sicilian, always a Sicilian. We keep the sun in our hearts."

But Francesca grew up in central Italy. Her father was senior military, and they moved every other year to Lazio, Umbria, and Perugia.

"Every summer we would go to my aunt and grandmother in Caltanissetta on a long summer holiday from June till September."

When it was time to begin at the university, Francesca moved back to Caltanissetta, and it was in Sicily she met "Tobbe," Torbjörn, who was there on holiday with an Italian friend.

"I visited Sweden that Christmas," Francesca tells us. "The following summer, 1989, we got married in Rome. It was 110 degrees out. Our honeymoon was to drive in a small convertible from Italy up to Sweden. When we arrived, it was 50 degrees out."

WITH THE SUN IN ONES HEART THE WINTERS ARE THE HARDEST.

"My restaurant is my way of getting through winter. Sweden is outside, and in here, I'm in Italy. With Italian food the Italian way."

"Many restaurants have made the food more Swedish. They serve pasta with a large piece of chicken or meat on top. That is like serving mackerel with strawberries."

At Francesca's they serve *antipasto*, primo, and *secondo*, the pasta on its own, the meat on its own, and the vegetables as a side on a separate plate.

"In Milan they work so much there is no time left to eat. They have therefore introduced *principale*, the main course. In Italy we do not eat main courses," Francesca says determinedly, "we eat in one way. Lunch, noon to 3 in the afternoon, maybe but not always *antipasto*, but *primo* and *secondo*."

Francesca is happy to have found that customers enjoy eating the Italian way. Not like Milan, but more like Sicily.

Francesca runs the restaurant That's Amore in Gothenburg with her husband, Tobbe. She's the boss in the kitchen, and he takes care of the floor. Their oldest daughter, Michelle, works in the kitchen as well and chats in Italian with her mother.

Caponata
Sweet and sour eggplant and bell pepper sauce, Sicily

This is a Sicilian classic, a typical summer dish that you always keep in the fridge and eat with a piece of bread. Celery heart is the inner, lighter part of the celery, which is not as woody. Simply remove the outer stalks (save for something else, for instance soup) and use the rest.

3 large eggplants
salt
3 large red bell peppers
3 small yellow onions
1 celery heart
olive oil
½ cup (1 dl) dry white wine
basil
3 large tomatoes
3.5 oz (100 g) black olives
3.5 oz (100 g) green olives
1 ½–2 tbsp capers
½ cup (1 dl) red wine vinegar
3.5 oz (100 g) sugar
3.5 oz (100 g) almonds
2.5 oz (70 g) pine nuts

Dice the eggplant in larger chunks. Sprinkle a generous amount of salt on top and place in a sieve under pressure—cover with a plate and set a bowl or saucepan with water on top. Let it drain for at least 30 minutes.

Spoon the salt off of the eggplant pieces and dry. Remove the cores of the bell peppers and dice. Finely chop the onions. Chop the celery.

Sauté the onion in olive oil until soft but without browning. Let the celery sauté with it after awhile. Add the wine and let it boil. Pour into a bowl and heat some oil in the pan.

Fry the bell peppers until soft and somewhat browned. Move into the bowl. Brown the eggplant chunks in olive oil. Make sure that they are dry before you place them in the pan, if not they will splash. If the heat is too low, they will become soggy and soft; if the temperature is to high, they will burn. They should have a nice golden color.

Fry in segments and move onto the bowl. Let a few leaves of basil fry with the eggplant. Place everything back in the pan.

Scald, peel, core, and dice the tomatoes and add to the pan. Add a handful of basil leaves as well. Add ripped green and black olives. Add capers. Brown while stirring. Add the red wine vinegar and sugar, blend well so that the sugar dissolves, and let it boil.

Scald and shell the almonds. Dry them off and chop or roughly grind in a food processor. Add pine nuts and almonds to the pan. Let cool. *Caponata* is best if it is allowed to rest for a while. Keep in the fridge.

Fagiolini alla fiorentina
Green beans with fennel, Tuscany

Use green beans or haricot verts (which are green beans harvested earlier). You may also use frozen beans. This side goes with most meals. In Italy they usually cook vegetables for a longer period of time than we regularly do, which makes them softer and the kick disappears. We actually don't cook haricot verts for a sufficient amount of time. A longer cooking time emphasizes the flavor.

1 lb (500 g) green beans or haricot verts
salt
1 yellow onion
olive oil
1 tsp fennel seeds
1 large plum tomato
black pepper

Boil the beans in salted water. Empty in a sieve and hold under cold running water to halt the cooking process. Let drain.

Finely chop the onion and sauté in olive oil with the fennel seeds until the onion is soft but without browning.

Scald, peel, core, and dice the tomatoes. Add to the pan and sauté. Stir now and then. The tomato should be soft, and the juice should boil away. Add the beans and simmer until they are warm. Season with salt and fresh ground black pepper.

Fagiolini all'aglio e mollica croccante
Green beans with bread crumbs, garlic, and parsley, Calabria

Mollica is simply the soft inner meat of the bread. *Crocanta* is crispy or crunchy. Bread crumbs fried in olive oil is one of the gems of the south Italian *cucina povera*, the poor man's kitchen. Used also in pasta dishes, it is sometimes called the poor man's Parmesan. Use day-old, dried country bread. Cut the crusts off and grate on a grater or use a food processor. Or use bought bread crumbs. This is a great side with grilled fish or meat. You can also finely chop a couple of anchovy fillets and let them sauté with the garlic.

1 lb (500 g) green beans or haricot verts
salt
1 garlic clove
1 handful leaf parsley
olive oil
¼ cup (½ dl) bread crumbs

Boil the beans in salted water. Empty in a sieve and hold under cold running water to halt the cooking process. Drain.

Finely chop the garlic and parsley and sauté in olive oil until the onion is soft without browning. Add the bread crumbs and fry until crunchy while stirring. Keep a close eye on it, because they brown quickly. Add the beans and warm. May be served warm or cold.

Fagiolini al tonno
Green beans with tuna, Lazio

This may also be served as an appetizer or a light lunch.

1.3 lbs (600 g) green beans or haricot verts
salt
14 oz (400 g) plum tomatoes
2 salad onions
1 can (½ lb (200 g) net weight) tuna in oil
1 handful leaf parsley
4 tbsp white wine vinegar
5 tbsp olive oil
salt
black pepper

Boil the beans in salted water. Empty in a sieve and hold under running cold water to halt the cooking process. Drain.

Core and dice the tomatoes. Rinse the salad onion and cut in thin circles. Let the oil drain off the tuna. Chop the parsley. Blend vinegar and oil in a large bowl. Season with salt and fresh ground pepper. Stir in half of the onion and half of the parsley. Fold the beans in and blend. Add the tomatoes and tuna.

Adjust the flavors with salt, black pepper, and vinegar or oil. It should have a fresh tart taste. Serve when the beans are still a little warm. Sprinkle the rest of the parsley and the onion on top before serving.

Fagilioni alla Genovese
Green beans with anchovies, Liguria

1 lb (500 g) green beans or haricot verts
3-4 anchovy fillets
1 handful leaf parsley
2 garlic cloves
olive oil
1 tbsp butter
salt
black pepper

Boil the beans for a few minutes in salted water. Empty in a sieve and hold under cool running water to halt the cooking process. Drain.

Rinse and dry the anchovies. Finely chop anchovies, parsley, and garlic. Heat oil and later melt the butter in the oil. Sauté anchovies, parsley, and garlic while stirring on low heat until the anchovies dissolve and the garlic is soft but not browned. Both anchovies and garlic are sensitive to heat.

Add the beans and let them warm carefully. Season with salt and fresh ground pepper. Goes with meat, fish, and fowl.

Fagioli all'uccelletto
White beans prepared like small fowl, Tuscany

This dish got its name from small birds and is also prepared this way, with garlic, sage, and tomatoes.

Beans are especially popular in Tuscany. So much so that other Italians will often call Tuscans *mangiafagioli*, bean eaters.

½ lb (250 g) dried large white beans or dried cannellini beans
3-4 plum tomatoes
3 garlic cloves
4-5 large sage leaves
4 tbsp olive oil
salt
black pepper

Rinse and soak the beans in a generous amount of water overnight.

Drain the soaking water. Place the beans in a large saucepan and cover the beans with water. Bring to a boil and then simmer the beans on low heat under a lid until soft, about 1 hour. Pour the water off and save for later.

Scald, peel, core, and dice the tomatoes. Chop the garlic and sage and sauté in olive oil until the garlic is soft and has browned somewhat. Add beans and tomatoes.

Season with salt and fresh ground pepper. Let everything boil for about 15-20 minutes. Add the saved boiling water if needed. Serve warm or at room temperature.

Indivia al forno
Endive au gratin

This is a side that works well with most things and may even work fine on its own as a small appetizer or with a cold cut.

4 endives
olive oil
1 small dried peperoncino
salt
black pepper
Parmesan
Bread crumbs

Set the oven to 430 F (220 C). Rinse the endives. Cut away any discolorations by the root. Remove any discolored or damaged leaves. Divide the endives lengthwise.

Butter an oven pan with some olive oil. Place the endives in the pan with the sliced sides facing upwards. Crumble some peperoncino on top.

Season with salt and black pepper. Drizzle some olive oil on top. Sprinkle some grated Parmesan. Sprinkle some bread crumbs. Cook the gratin to a nice color. Serve warm or cold.

Finocchio al forno
Fennel au gratin

1-2 fennel
olive oil
1 small dried peperoncino
salt
black pepper
Parmesan
bread crumbs

The fennel can be cooked the same way as the endives. Wash and cut the fennel in smaller pieces; cut smaller fennel in half and larger fennel in quarts. Do not remove the inner root. Boil al dente in salted water. Pour the water off and dry with paper towels. Continue as you did with the endives.

Scorzonera fritta
Fried salsify, Liguria

Salsify is also called "the poor man's asparagus" and is a delicious winter delicacy.

1.5 lbs (750 g) salsify
juice from 1 lemon or white wine vinegar
salt
2 eggs
¾ cup (1 ½ dl) flour
2 tbsp grated Parmesan
2 tbsp dry white wine
¼ cup (½ dl) water
oil for frying

Peel the salsify with a potato peeler under running water. Cut into 1–1 ½ inch long pieces and place in cold water with lemon and vinegar, otherwise they will darken. Boil until soft in salted water; they should maintain some resistance, about 10-15 minutes. Another way to peel salsify is to boil them in salted water with the peel still on for a few minutes, Spoon them into cold water, and scrape the peel off with a knife. Cut them to the right size and finish boiling. The preparation will then be quicker.

Separate the egg whites from the yolks. Whisk yolks, flour, Parmesan, white wine, and water. Whisk the egg whites stiff and fold in with the yolk blend.

Heat frying oil in a saucepan to 350 F (180 C) (or until it takes a small piece of bread about 30 seconds to turn brown).

Drain the salsify and dry them with paper towels. Dip the pieces in the batter and fry until golden. Let them drain on paper. Serve right away.

Scorzonera in umido
Fricassee of salsify, Liguria

A lemon fresh stew made with eggs. This cannot be compared to a regular meal stew; it both fresher and more delicious.

1 ½ cups (750 g) salsify
juice of 1 lemon or white wine vinegar
1 yellow onion
1 handful leaf parsley
4 tbsp olive oil
salt
1 tsp flour
1–2 cups cups (2–4 dl) bouillon, vegetable or chicken
2 yolks
juice of ½ a lemon

Peel the salsify with a potato peeler under running water. Cut in 1-1/2 inch long pieces and place in cold water with lemon juice or vinegar.

Finely chop the onion. Finely chop half of the parsley. Sauté onion and parsley in olive oil in a wide saucepan without browning the onion.

Drain the water off the salsify and place in the saucepan. Let them brown for a few minutes. Add flour and stir. Cover with bouillon. Simmer until the salsify is soft, but still maintains some resistance, about 10-15 minutes.

Whisk the yolks with the juice of ½ a lemon and ¼ cup (½ dl) bouillon. Stir in with the ingredients in the saucepan. The sauce should not boil. Sprinkle the rest of the parsley on top and serve.

Pomodori essiccati al forno
Oven dried tomatoes

Sundried tomatoes are a way of preserving abundant harvests from the summer. It is a simple preserving method, but also a sort of preparation since it both emphasizes and concentrates the flavors.

Many dry the tomatoes themselves outside in the garden on a kitchen towel and covered with a mosquito net so as to prevent insects from enjoying the delicious meal.

To dry the tomatoes in the oven is not as charming, but it tastes great. Use the tomatoes in salads, as a snack, or in focaccia before you bake it. The more flavorful the tomatoes are, the better they turn out dried.

½ lb (300 g) tomatoes, cherry, cocktail or romantic
1 tsp salt
1 tsp sugar
1 tsp dried rosemary or thyme

Preheat the oven to 440 F (225 C).

Cut the tomatoes in half across; feel free to leave the stalks on.

Place the tomatoes on a piece of parchment paper on a baking sheet with the cut side facing upward.

Sprinkle salt, sugar, and spices on top. Place the plate in the oven and bake for about 1 ½ hours. The time may vary depending on the size of the tomatoes.

Carcicofi alla romana
Braised Jerusalem artichokes, Lazio

The large, round Jerusalem artichokes of spring, *carciofi romaneschi*, that they serve at most restaurants when they're in season, are especially good in this dish. Traditionally, they should be stuffed with wild mint, *mentuccia*, but regular mint works fine as well.

4 Jerusalem artichokes
juice of 1 lemon
3 tbsp chopped mint
1 tbsp chopped leaf parsley
1–2 chopped garlic cloves
1 tbsp olive oil
½ cup (1 dl) dry white wine
½ cup (1 dl) water
5 tbsp olive oil
½ lemon
salt

Remove the thick outer leaves of the Jerusalem artichokes. Groom the stalks and leave about 2 inches. Rub the artichokes with half a lemon so that they do not discolor.

Cut across the artichokes right above the small indent so that the rough upper part of the leaf falls away. The artichokes should be able to balance on the cut surface with the stalk pointing upwards. Place the artichokes in a bowl with water and lemon.

Blend mint, leaf parsley, and garlic with about 1 tbsp olive oil. Do one artichoke at a time. Open the flower, scoop the threads away with a teaspoon, and replace with some of the herb blend.

Place the artichokes in a deep saucepan with the stalks pointing upward. Add water, wine, and the remaining oil. Add ½ lemon and season with salt. Cover with a lid, bring to a boil, and let it carefully simmer for about 1 hour. Cool before serving.

Carciofi alla giuda
Jerusalem artichokes the Jewish way, Lazio

Jerusalem artichokes are thistle flowers that are harvested right before blossoming. At street markets you can find rinsed Jerusalem artichokes soaked in lemon water. The top artichokes, *cimaroli*, are considered the finest kind, since they arrive first. These firstborns are more expensive and are sold in singles and not in a bunch. *Braccioli* grow further down and are not as popular.

8 Jerusalem artichokes
the juice of 1 lemon
salt
black pepper
olive oil
sea salt

Remove the outer hard leaves and the hard tops on the other leaves. When you' re done, the top looks like a flower.

Rub the artichokes with a lemon and place them in lemon water to avoid discoloration. Lift each artichoke, shake the water out, dry it well, and open it with your fingers. Press each against the sink so that they open even more. Season with salt and ground black pepper.

Cover the artichoke halfway with olive oil in a saucepan. Heat the oil carefully. The temperature is right when a small piece of bread turns brown in 30 minutes. Carefully add one artichoke to the oil. Use a wooden ladle. Fry for about 10 minutes. Turn it so that the other side may fry for 10 minutes as well. The leaves should be brown and crispy.

Lift them up and splash some water on them to force the oil out. Set them with the flower facing downward on a paper towel to drain. Crumble sea salt on top and serve.

Parmigiana di melanzane
Eggplant casserole with mozzarella and Parmesan, Campania

A much-loved dish that exists in many varieties in southern Italy. Sometimes you may find a blend of eggplant slices that are roasted in the oven and grilled.

3 eggplants
salt
1 garlic clove
olive oil
1 lb (500 g) strained tomatoes
basil
4.4 oz (125 g) mozzarella
Parmesan
bread crumbs

Set the oven to 440 F (225 C). Cut the eggplants in about ¼ inch thick slices, lengthwise.

Drain by either warming them on full heat in the microwave for a few minutes until they let go of the water or sprinkling a generous amount of salt on top and placing them in a sieve under pressure—cover with a plate and set a bowl or saucepan with water on top. Let it drain for at least 30 minutes.

Rinse the salt off and dry. While the eggplants are draining, make the tomato sauce.

Crush and peel the garlic clove. Sauté until soft without browning in olive oil. Add the strained tomatoes

and a few basil leaves and let it simmer until the sauce thickens. Its texture should be similar to vanilla cream.

Heat a generous amount of olive oil in a frying pan. Fry a couple of eggplant slices at a time until golden. Let them drain on paper towels.

Place a layer of eggplant slices in the bottom of a baking pan. Cover with tomato sauce. Add basil leaves. Slice the mozzarella thinly or dice. Distribute on top. Sprinkle freshly grated Parmesan. Continue in multiple layers. Finish with tomato sauce and Parmesan. Sprinkle bread crumbs on top and bake to a nice color. This dish is commonly served at room temperature, but also tastes good warm.

Asparagi alla parmigiana
Green asparagus with Parmesan and butter, Emilie-Romagna

A simple way of serving primeurs, *primeze*. You can prepare, for instance, broccoli, beans, green beans, haricot verts, and cauliflower the same way.

1 lb (500 g) asparagus
salt
3 tbsp butter
black pepper
1.7 oz (50 g) Parmesan

Set the oven to 390 F (200 C). Break off the lower part of the asparagus. When you bend the asparagus, you will naturally find the spot it should break. Throw the bottom piece out.

Place the asparagus in a saucepan and barely cover them with water. Remove the asparagus and bring the water to a boil. Add salt and place the asparagus back in the saucepan. Boil until they bend easily when you lift them by their ends, about 5 minutes. Empty the asparagus in a sieve and spoon with cold water to cool.

Dry them and place in a greased baking pan. Add some spoonfuls of butter, lightly salt, add ground black pepper, and sprinkle grated Parmesan on top. Bake in the oven until golden. Serve right away.

PANE E PIZZE *bread & pizza*

Bread is a central part of Italian food. No meal is served without bread. Bread is a snack while you wait. Something to taste the olive oil with. Something to make the appetizer with. Something to dip in your soup that soaks up the last bit of pasta sauce or broth.

It is such a commodity to clean the plate with a piece of bread that this last bread piece has received a name of its own. It is called *scarpetta,* which means small shoe.

Bread is also a part of one of the foods that people associate with Italy—the pizza. To Italians, eating pizza is the essential image of enjoying food with your friends—a simple and unpretentious way to hang out. Bread should be shared with friends. "Companion" is who we share bread with, after the Latin *cum pane. Compagnone* is a social, outgoing person; *compagno* is a friend and a comrade.

There is a deep-rooted tradition in Italy to never throw out old bread, but rather use it in other dishes.

Bread is loaded with symbolic meaning, not least because of its role in Christianity. It is common to bless bread dough during baking.

ITALIAN BREAD

It used to be common to bake homemade bread in a shared oven. People didn't have their own ovens in their homes, so they walked with the baking sheet down to the shared city oven or the local bakery. It is still like this in smaller communities.

Today people don't bake much at home. And why would you when there's a bakery on every corner? Even the *supermercati* receive daily deliveries of fresh bread from local bakeries. The industrial plastic bag bread is just not seen, except for sandwich bread.

White bread is the most common, although an increasing knowledge has made breads rich in fiber more popular. Earlier, all bread used to be high in fiber, and only the rich ate white bread. When it later became possible for the general population to eat white bread, everyone, quite understandable, wanted to be like the rich. The white bread is often rich in flavor and has a lovely chewy texture as a result of long rising and the use of sourdough.

Sourdough is called *lievito di madre* or *pasta acida*. *Biga* is a starting dough that is made the day before and is left to rise overnight before it is worked in with another dough. You can also take a *madre* from a finished dough and use it in the next dough. Take ½ lb (200 g) of dough, place it in a plastic bowl with a lid, and leave in the fridge. This bit of dough can later be the basis of the next dough, which you also save ½ lb (200 g) of, and so on . . . If you want to take a break from the baking, you can freeze the piece of dough and take it out when you need it.

Pane bianco con biga
White bread with biga

0.7 oz (20 g) fresh yeast
1 ½ cups (3 dl) water
1 lb (450 g) wheat flour special
2 tsp salt
½ lb (200 g) biga, see recipe below
olive oil

Dissolve the yeast in the water. Stir in the flour and the salt. Work into dough. Then work the biga in with the dough. Knead the dough until it doesn't stick, is elastic, and bounces back when you poke it, about 15 minutes.

Lightly oil a bowl. Roll the dough around so that it is covered in oil and leave it in the bowl. Cover with a kitchen towel or plastic wrap and let it rise for 1 hour. Press the dough down, cover once more and let it rise for another hour.

Shape the dough into a ball and place on a floured piece of parchment paper. Sprinkle with flour, cover with a kitchen towel, and let it rise to double its size, about 1 hour.

Set the oven to 480 F (250 C). Place a baking stone in the middle of the oven or use a baking pan upside down. Pour a couple of tablespoons of water in a pie dish and place it at the bottom of the oven. Slide the bread from the baking sheet onto the hot rock or baking pan.

Lower the heat to 390 F (200 C) after 5 minutes. Open the oven door and release some of the heat after another 10 minutes. Continue to open every 5 minutes. Bake for 30–35 minutes altogether. Let the bread cool on a baking grid. For an extra hard and crunchy crust, you can splash some water on the bread with a flower sprayer right before you take it out.

Biga:

½ tsp fresh yeast
¾ cup (1 ½ dl) water
½ lb (250 g) wheat flour

Dissolve the yeast in the water. Stir in the flour. Cover with plastic wrap and let it rise overnight at room temperature. The next day your biga is ready.

Pane Bianco
White bread

This is a dough that takes care of itself. Blend it and let it rise overnight or through a workday. Then you can bake one large bread, a smaller *Panini*, or a few *ciabatte* with the dough. I prefer measuring the water and flour on an electric scale. It is both quick and exact. Although exact is not really that important, since the flour may act differently from one time to another. How much water it binds may depend on air humidity and other elements, so you still have to wait and see. The important thing is to dare to make the dough moist, almost wet. This means it's harder to work with, but it also makes a light and airy bread. Then dare to let it rise for a long time, and you'll end up with a very nice bread.

½ tsp fresh yeast or ½ tsp dry yeast
½ lb (300 g) (1 ½ cups [3 dl]) cold water
1 ½ tsp salt
1–2 tbsp olive oil (optional)
0.8 lbs (390 g) (3 ¼ cups [6 ½ dl]) wheat flour

Dissolve the yeast in cold water. Stir in salt and optionally stir in olive oil. Then slowly stir in the flour and work into dough with a wooden ladle. Cover the bowl with plastic wrap and let it rise for 10 minutes.

Place a generous amount of flour on the table and empty the dough on top. Dip your hands in water so the dough won't stick to your fingers. Pull the dough out to a large square. Then fold the sides in so that it becomes a square of about 10x10 inches. Turn the package so that the joint is facing downwards. Cover the top with flour and let it rise for 45—60 minutes under a kitchen towel.

Panini: Heat the oven to the highest possible temperature (480–530 F [250–275 C]). Leave a baking stone in the oven if you have one. If not, let a baking pan stand upside down in the middle of the oven (if it is upside down, it is easier to slide the bread on and off).

Divide the dough in elongated pieces with a dough scraper. Separate them and divide into smaller breads. Place on a piece of parchment paper. Pour a few tablespoons of water in a pie dish that you don't care about

(because it will, in time, be quite tarnished) and place it at the bottom of the oven. (The steam that forms makes the bread rise better in the oven and helps make a crispy crust.)

Slide the bread onto the hot pan in the oven with the help of a pizza plate or tray upside down. Bake until golden, about 15–20 minutes. If you think the bread is gaining color very quickly ,you can lower the temperature slightly. After 10 minutes, open the oven door and let the steam out. Feel free to open the door a few times more during baking. Let the bread cool on a baking grid.

Ciabatta: Heat the oven to the highest possible temperature (480–530 F [250–275 C]). Divide the dough in elongated pieces with a dough scraper. Separate them and divide in smaller breads. Place on a piece of parchment paper. Bake the same way as the panini. Let the bread cool on a baking grid.

Filone, larger bread: Warm the oven to 480 F (250 C). Turn the dough so that the joint is facing upwards and place on a piece of parchment paper. In the process, you may also shape it a little.

Bake like the panini, with a stone or a baking pan upside down and water in a pie dish. Bake for about 30–35 minutes. Open the door for airing after about 15 minutes. Then every 5 minutes. Let the bread cool on a baking grid.

Grissini toriniesi
Breadsticks, Piedmont

In Turin they have baked these thin breadsticks since the 1300s. Vary with different added flavors. Roll in sesame seeds or finely chopped rosemary. Or blend finely chopped sage or grated Parmesan in the dough.

0.5 oz (15 g) yeast or ½ tsp dry yeast
water
1 lb 475 g (almost 3 ½ cups (7 dl)) wheat flour
1 tsp salt
durum wheat flour
olive oil

Dissolve the yeast in 4 tablespoons of water. Add a sufficient amount of flour so that the dough becomes moist. Cover with a kitchen towel and let it rise until it starts bubbling.

Pour the remaining flour in a bowl. Add the salt. Pour in room temperature water and blend into soft dough. You need about 1 ³/₈–1 ¹/₃ cups (2 ³/₄–3 ¹/₄ dl) water. Then work in the starter dough and knead in a machine or by hand until the dough is elastic and soft and bounces back when you poke it, about 10 minutes. Shape into a bun, pat it all over with olive oil, and let it rise in a bowl under a kitchen towel to double its size, about 2 hours.

Sprinkle durum wheat on the baking table. There are two ways you can make the sticks. Either take small pieces of the dough and roll them out into thin sticks on the table with your hands or roll out a thin sheet on the baking table and later cut into thin sticks. Place the sticks on parchment paper and let them rise under a kitchen towel for 1 hour.

Set the oven to 390 F (200 C).

Bake in the oven for 20 minutes. Cool on a baking grid.

Focaccia al rosmarino
Focaccia with rosemary, Liguria

In Liguria, they eat focaccia everywhere, and you see it all over—for breakfast, for lunch, and for a snack. But similar breads are also popular in other parts of Italy. In Tuscany, it is called *schiacciata* and is sometimes flavored with red grapes. In Piedmont, they use anchovies and walnuts. In Apulia, ripe cherry tomatoes, oregano, and olives provide extra flavor.

Instead of rosemary, you can also use fresh thyme or small pieces of onion. Make sure that you really stick the spices in the bread so that the flavors spread properly. Spices that are sticking out will easily burn.

0.5 oz (15 g) yeast or ½ tsp dry yeast
1 tsp sugar
1 ¼ cups (2 ½ dl) water
14 oz (400 g) (about 3 ¼ cups [6 ½]) wheat flour
1 tsp salt
½ cup (1 dl) olive oil
fresh rosemary
salt flakes

Dissolve the yeast with the sugar in cold water. Let it sit until it starts bubbling.

Blend flour and salt in a bowl. Add the yeast blend and half of the olive oil and work into dough. Knead in a machine or by hand until it is elastic and bounces back when you poke it. Shape into a bun, pat it with olive oil all over, and let it rise in a bowl under a kitchen towel to double its size, about 2 hours.

Push the dough down to the original size. Grease a metal oven pan, about 8x12 inches, with olive oil. Arrange the dough in the pan. Cover with plastic wrap and let it rise to almost double its size, about 30–40 minutes.

Set the oven to 430 F (220 C).

Poke holes in the surface of the bread with your index finger. Fill with small rosemary sprigs. Brush with the remaining olive oil and sprinkle with generous amounts of salt flakes. Bake until golden, about 20 minutes. Turn out and cool on a baking grid.

Amelia Adamo

AMELIA ADAMO'S EYES STILL SHINE WITH LOVE.

"I have newly gained a greater relation to Italian food," she says. "I have met an Italian man that very much enjoys cooking. His name is Lucio, and his food almost makes me teary eyed as I remember my mother's food."

There is one strong food memory from her childhood that often resurfaces. Amelia Adamo was 6 years old and was attending a convent school. She was only allowed to come home and meet her mother, Elda, during the weekends. She and her stepfather, Oscar Adamo, as well as many other Italians, lived at a boarding house because they couldn't rent a place of their own.

"I came home and spaghetti would be hanging to dry all over the kitchen," Amelia tells us. "On the stove, a pot of onions, carrots, celery, prime rib, and tomatoes would be boiling. The aluminum saucepan was gigantic because it had so many mouths to feed."

Back then Amelia was only allowed to eat Italian during the weekends. The nuns at convent school were German.

"We ate a lot of dumplings and things like that . . . it was a terrible time."

But from age 11, the only food that counted was Italian food. Her mother made Roman food, and it was in Rome, in Lazio, Amelia was born. Roman food is still her favorite.

"I love the simple pasta dishes. *Cacio e pepe* and *aglio, olio e peperoncino*. And Lucio makes a wonderful *pasta alla vongole*. Carpaccio is delicious as well, the original on ox fillets or tuna fillets."

AMELIA SEEMS LIKE SHE'S BECOMING MORE AND MORE ITALIAN each year.

"It is the knowledge. I have been devoted to dig into my roots, and I often travel to Italy."

And Italians talk food:

"There is so much delicious food. Tasty vegetable dishes. The way the meat is prepared. Thin slices of veal

Amelia Adamo is a Swedish media mogul and the brain and heart behind such successes as Amelia, Tara and M-Magasinet where she is often seen on the cover. She has received "Stora Journalistpriset" twice.

that are grilled and just flavored with a tad bit of lemon. It's the simplicity . . ."

"The raw materials are flavorful, the olive oil is good, the bread you break with it …They don't set the table nicely in the restaurants, there are crumbs on the tables, wine is served in milk glasses or small thick wine glasses, the food is not arranged in a pretty manner, and we never all receive the food at the same time. There is no finesse, but the food is extremely central for how they feel. They know the art of enjoying and the art of socializing."

Pizzette
Mini Pizzas

"I have served these multiple times through the years," Amelia says. "It tastes good and it is not at all pretentious." Bake into really small *pizette* or somewhat larger. The larger ones are best warm, the smaller are tasty cold as well. Perfect with a bubbly glass of prosecco.

1 batch pizza dough, see
p.168
durum wheat flour
strained tomatoes
mozzarella
Parmesan
anchovies
capers
black pepper
olive oil
preserved Jerusalem
artichokes
arugula
basil
leaf parsley

Make the pizza dough. Set the oven to the highest temperature, hot air if you have that setting and it gets even warmer. Place a baking stone in the oven if you have one. If not, use a baking pan upside down in the middle of the oven.

Small pizzette: Roll the dough out thinly on a baking table that is covered with durum wheat. This flour is a bit rougher than the common wheat flour and is easier to work with; it also makes for a nicer surface on the pizza. Cut small rounds with a glass or a round cookie cutter.
Larger pizzette: Divide the dough into smaller pieces and roll out small pizzas.

Pizza 1: Cover with a thin layer of strained tomatoes. Add mozzarella in small dices and fresh grated Parmesan.
Pizza 2: Cover with a thin layer of strained tomatoes. Rinse and dry the anchovy fillets and capers and place on top. Add mozzarella and Parmesan.
Pizza 3: Cover with a thin layer of strained tomatoes. Add diced mozzarella and fresh grated Parmesan—the rest will be added after baking.

Season with fresh ground black pepper and drizzle some olive oil over all the pizzas. Bake to a nice color in the oven. Place the Jerusalem artichokes and arugula on some of the tomato pizzas and basil leaves on the others. Add leaf parsley and basil on top of the anchovy pizzas.

ITALIAN PIZZA

The communal agreement is that you eat pizza late at night when you don't want a large meal. Places that serve pizza at other times of the day will name the pizza appropriately: *pizza per pranzo*, pizza for lunch.

In contrast to pasta, pizza is rarely made at home. You eat pizza out with friends; it is cheap and therefore popular among the youth. Many holes in the wall sell *pizza rustica* or *pizza al taglio*, thicker pizza baked on large plates and cut into bites for eating on the street.

Naples is usually called the birthplace of pizza, no less so by the Neapolitans themselves, but it is not that simple. Pizza definitely belongs to all of southern Italy, from Rome to the south. The Romans made a flat bread called *picea*. Pizza from different parts of the country may vary. In Rome, they want it thinner and harder. In Naples, it has a thicker crust and is both softer and thicker than in Rome.

A real pizza oven should be a wood burner and very hot, over 400 C, in Naples 485 C. This is not possible in our kitchens, but use as much heat as possible. A baking stone or a pizza stone also helps make the pizza crispy. Leave it in the oven for a long time so that it really heats up. If you don't have a stone, you can leave a baking sheet in the oven to heat. Turn it upside down, and it will be easier to slide the pizza on and off. Place the pizzas on parchment paper, and they're even easier to handle.

Use the tomato sauce sparingly: a few tablespoons for a regular-sized pizza and spread it thinly. Too much sauce and the crust becomes soft and doughy. Don't make it complicated. Italian food is about simplicity. Strained tomatoes of good quality are fine as a tomato sauce. There's no need to season it.

Dice or slice mozzarella in good time so that it has time to drain off a bit. Mozzarella will often have a lot of fluids, especially if you use a fresh buffalo mozzarella. You don't want those fluids on your pizza.

Impasto per la pizza
Pizza dough

This is our favorite dough. It makes thin, crispy pizzas, a little more like Rome than Naples. If you have an old baking machine, you can use the dough program to make the dough. Just add the ingredients according to the instructions, set the timer, and it will be ready when you get home from work.

About 4 regular-sized pizzas:

1 tbsp olive oil
1 ½ cups (3 dl) cold water
2 tsp (10 g) fresh yeast or 1 tsp dry yeast
1 lb (500 g) (nearly 4 ¼ cups (8 ½ dl)) wheat flour
durum wheat flour for rolling out

Blend the oil and the cold water in a bowl. Dissolve the yeast in the water. Stir in the flour. Work into dough. Knead it until smooth and shiny, preferably 15–20 minutes. Work the salt into the dough when you are about halfway through. Salt prevents gluten threads, therefore we add it a little later. Cover with plastic wrap or a kitchen towel and let it rise to twice its size, 2–3 hours.

You can make the dough in the morning, push it down later when you get home, and let it rise again. Don't be afraid to let the dough rise for too long; it only gets better. When you press the dough down, it will start rising again without the danger of spilling over the edge.

You may also make the dough at night and let it rise slowly in the fridge overnight, press it down in the morning, and let it continue to rise.

Knead the dough right before you roll it out into pizzas. Then let it rise for an additional 15 minutes. Divide in 4 equally sized pieces and roll out into pizzas on a baking table covered with durum wheat.

Pizza Margherita

The queen of pizzas, named after the first queen of Italy. Created in Naples on June 11, 1889, under a marble plate at the Pizzeria Brandi (which at the time had a different name *Pietro . . . e basta cosi*, Pietro . . .and that's enough). This is often made with *fior di latte*, in other words, mozzarella made with cow's milk since buffalo mozzarella usually holds so much liquid. Fresh basil is a must (don't even consider dried).

Italian food culture is packed with anecdotes about the beginning of food dishes that are often not completely true. That Margherita got its name to honor the queen is true. But it's also true that the combination of tomato, mozzarella, and basil had been used before. We use some fresh grated Parmesan as well.

tomatoes: strained, whole in a can, fresh plum tomatoes (preferably San Marzano), or fresh cherry tomatoes

4.4 oz (125 g) mozzarella for 4 pizzas
fresh basil
Parmesan
salt
black pepper
olive oil

Roll out the pizzas. Cover with a thin layer of strained tomatoes; core canned tomatoes, drain well, cut in shreds, and arrange on the pizzas; scald, peel, core, drain, and shred fresh plum tomatoes and arrange; or cut the cherry tomatoes in half and squeeze the liquid out before you add them to the pizzas.

Slice or dice the mozzarella. Let them drain well. Arrange on the pizzas. Grate a few basil leaves and arrange on top. Add fresh grated Parmesan. Season with salt and fresh ground black pepper. Drizzle olive oil on top and bake.

Garnish with fresh basil leaves and serve.

Pizza marinara

One of the two classic pizzas of Naples. The other is Margherita. In other places, a marinara is a pizza packed with seafood, but not in Naples. It is said that this is what the starving fishermen would order after a night at sea. They wanted the one that was ready in the shortest amount of time—garlic, oregano, and oil. Or it was the pizza they made at sea where they didn't have fresh mozzarella.

tomatoes: strained, whole in a can, fresh plum tomatoes
(preferably San Marzano), or fresh cherry tomatoes
garlic
oregano, dry or fresh
salt
olive oil

Roll out the pizzas. Cover with a thin layer of strained tomatoes; core canned tomatoes, drain well, cut in shreds, and arrange on the pizzas; scald, peel, core, drain, and shred fresh plum tomatoes and arrange; or cut the cherry tomatoes in half and squeeze the liquid out before you add them to the pizzas.

Peel and thinly slice the garlic cloves. Arrange a few slices on each pizza. Sprinkle oregano on top. Add salt and drizzles of olive oil. Bake.

Calzone
Folded baked pizza

Fill for 2 pizzas:

1.7 oz (50 g) mozzarella
0.8 oz (25 g) boiled ham
0.8 (25 g) salami
1 egg
salt
black pepper
0.8 oz (25 g) ricotta

Dice the mozzarella and let it drain well. Dice ham and salami. Blend mozzarella, salami and ham in a bowl. Whisk an egg and work in with the blend. Season with salt and ground black pepper. Add the ricotta. Scoop the filling onto one side of the pizzas. Fold the other half over the filling so that it looks like a half-moon. Knead the dough together along the seam. Bake.

Pizza alla romana

Pizza names can be a tad bit confusing. In Naples this is *alla romana*, as in Rome, and in Rome it is called *alle napoletana*, as in Naples.

tomatoes: strained, whole in a can, fresh plum tomatoes
(preferably San Marzano), or fresh cherry tomatoes
anchovies
capers
4.4 oz (125 g) mozzarella for 4 pizzas
Parmesan
salt
black pepper
olive oil
fresh basil

Roll out the pizzas. Cover with a thin layer of strained tomatoes; core canned tomatoes, drain well, cut in shreds, and arrange on the pizzas; scald, peel, core, drain, and shred fresh plum tomatoes and arrange; or cut the cherry tomatoes in half and squeeze the liquid out before you add them to the pizzas.

Rinse and dry the anchovy fillets. Arrange them whole on the pizzas or cut them in smaller pieces and arrange. Rinse, dry, and arrange the capers.

Slice or dice the mozzarella. Let it drain well. Arrange on the pizzas. Add fresh grated Parmesan. Season with salt and ground black pepper. Drizzle olive oil on top and bake. Garnish with fresh basil leaves and serve.

Pizza Bianca
White Pizza

We first discovered this variety of the *pizza Bianca* at the beach in Positano. Try to get ahold of Italian boiled ham, *prosciutto cotto*. It is delicious. Instead of ham, you can top it off with grilled eggplant in olive oil after baking. In many places, *pizza Bianca* is a pizza with just mozzarella. It is one of the most common children's pizzas and the name is short for *Bianca Neve*, which means Snow White.

garlic
sliced boiled ham
salt
slack pepper
4.4 oz (125 g) mozzarella for 4 pizzas
Parmesan
olive oil
arugula (optional)

Peel and thinly slice the garlic. Arrange a few slices on each pizza. Arrange boiled ham on the pizzas. Season with salt and ground black pepper.

Slice or dice the mozzarella. Let it drain well. Arrange on the pizzas. Add fresh grated Parmesan. Season with salt and ground black pepper. Drizzle olive oil on top and bake. If you wish, you can rinse and dry fresh arugula and add to the pizza before serving.

Pizza fritta
Fried pizza

Small pizette fried in a pan. Simple and sinfully good.

pizza dough
olive oil
strained tomatoes
Parmesan
fresh basil

Roll the dough out very thinly. Make rounds with a glass. Poke the rounds with a fork.

Heat olive oil in a frying pan. Fry the small pizzas until golden on both sides. Let them drain on a kitchen towel. Cover with a thin layer of strained tomatoes. Top with fresh grated Parmesan and basil and serve right away.

Other classic pizzas:

Capricciosa (means imaginative): mozzarella, mushrooms, Jerusalem artichokes, boiled ham, olives
Quattro stagioni (the four seasons): commonly the same ingredients as capricciosa, but in sections instead of mixed
Quattro formaggi (four cheeses): provolone, Parmesan, pecorino, gruyere
Diavola (Develish, hot): tomato, mozzarella, strong salami, oregano
Siciliana (Sicilian): mozzarella, eggplant, zucchini, bell peppers

DOLCI *desserts & sweets*

Dolci is a nice little word. It means smooth, mild, gentle, delightful, and lovable. And it means sweet. As in desserts.

But *dolci* stills plays a rather small role in Italy. This is not because they avoid the sweets. You can just glance at an Italian breakfast to know that that's not the case. They are just not as excited about sweets after eating.

The most common dessert is the ripe fruit of the season—sliced or mixed as a fruit salad, *Macedonia.*

Rich tart-like cakes and pies are eaten at the restaurant or bought at the bakery and brought home, *la pasticceria.* Ricotta and mascarpone are more common than cream.

They serve ice cream as a dessert as well, but first and foremost they eat ice cream during their night walk, *la passegiata*, where you show your face and look at others.

Cookies are for breakfast or for dipping in espresso or wine. Hazelnuts are added for flavor in the north, and almonds in the south.

Torta caprese
Almond and chocolate cake, Campania

The little island outside of Naples has not only given Italy the much-loved salad with mozzarella, tomato, and basil, but also this delicious cake, both an almond cake and a chocolate cake. Sometimes it is also called *torta alla mandorle*. You see it everywhere in Campania, in Naples, along the Amalfi coast, and in Salerno. They will often powder the powdered sugar on top of the cake through a stencil so that the cake reads Capri or Caprese. Worth mentioning: Despite its height, this cake is without flour, starch, or baking powder. It is not difficult to make, but you need a lot of different bowls.

11 oz (340 g) almonds
3 x 2 tbsp sugar

½ lb (225 g) dark chocolate of good quality
1 cup (225 g) butter

6 eggs
¾ cup (1 ½ dl) sugar

powdered sugar

Set the oven to 300 F (150 C). Fasten a piece of parchment paper between the bottom and the ring in a spring pan, about 9.5 inches in diameter. Butter, sprinkle with flour, and shake off any surplus flour.

Scald and peel the almonds. Place them in boiling water and boil for a few minutes. Move them under cold water and squeeze the almonds out of their shells. Dry the almonds with paper towels. Roast them in a dry pan. Let cool.

Grind the almonds in a food processor. First pour ⅓ of the almonds and 2 tbsp sugar into a bowl. Repeat twice with the remaining thirds.

Chop the chocolate and place it in a bowl or a small saucepan. Place that in a water bath in a larger saucepan. Warm and melt the chocolate while stirring. Add the butter and melt while stirring.

Separate the egg whites from the yolks. Place the yolks in a large bowl. Whisk with an electric beater into a light and fluffy foam, about 5 minutes. Whisk in ¾ cup (1 ½ dl) sugar a little at the time. Whisk the chocolate blend in with the yolks. Blend well. Fold in the ground almonds with a silicone spatula.

Whisk egg whites and 1/4 cup (1/2 dl) sugar to a hard foam in a separate bowl. Carefully turn the egg foam in the chocolate blend with a silicone spatula in two rounds: fold in half of the egg white foam and blend well before you add the other half. Make sure that it all blends well. Do not whisk, but fold it in. If you whisk, the air will disappear from the batter.

Pour the batter into the spring form. Bake on a baking sheet in the bottom part of the oven for about 1 ½ hours. The cake is ready when nothing sticks to the test stick. Cool on a baking grid.

When the cake is cool, flip it out on a serving plate and remove the ring and bottom. The top of the cake is now the bottom. Sprinkle powdered sugar on top and serve.

Cassata al forno
Homemade cassata, Sicily

Also called *cassata catanese* after the city of Catania, this is the homemade variety of this classic cake. It is easy to make and tastes amazingly good. Traditionally you should use Sicilian ricotta made of cow's milk. When that is not possible, a hung cow's milk ricotta is fine, in other words, a ricotta that is hung to drain for 24 hours or so.

The flavors in the cake are reminiscent of the more famous *cassata alla siciliana*, where you combine a sugar cake with ricotta cream, cover it with marzipan, and decorate with beautiful candied fruits. *Cassata alla siciliana* is rarely made at home, even in Sicily. You buy the cake at the local bakery, *pasticceria*. *Cassata gelata* is the ice cream that's flavored with candied fruits.

Just like many Italian dishes with a strong position in the Italian culture, there are stories of *cassata* that brings it all the way back to the Arabic rule of the island. And just like the other stories, you should take them with a grain of salt. Closer study makes it clear that *cassata* as a dessert has a quite short history, even if the flavors have ties to the Arabic times. *Cassata al forno* is rich, and a small piece will do.

Pasta frola, pie dough:
6 tbsp melted butter
½ lb (210 g) (1 ¾ cups (3 ½ dl)) flour
5 oz (135 g) (¾ cup (1 ½ dl)) sugar
2 tsp baking powder
½ tsp vanilla sugar
2 eggs
1 tsp grated lemon zest

Crema di ricotta, ricotta filling:
1 lb (500 g) ricotta
3.5 oz (100 g) (just more than ½ cup (1 dl)) sugar
½ tsp vanilla sugar
¼ cup (½ dl) chopped dark chocolate
¼ cup (½ dl) succade

powdered sugar

Melt the butter and let it cool. Sift the flour. Blend it with sugar, baking powder, and vanilla sugar in a bowl.

In a separate bowl, blend eggs and lemon zest (without the white). Make an indent in the flour and pour in some egg that you blended with a fork. Continue blending the eggs in with the flour, a little at a time. Work into a crumbly dough. Work the melted butter in the same way you did the eggs. Powder flour on the baking table and quickly work into a very loose dough. Do not knead. Cover in plastic wrap and place in the fridge overnight.

You may also make the dough in a food processor. Place milk, sugar, baking powder, lemon zest, and butter in the mixer and mix quickly. Whisk the eggs lightly in a bowl and add a little at a time while the mixer is still running. Quickly work into dough.

Place a small kitchen towel in a thread sieve. Place the ricotta in the towel and squeeze and twist around so that the ricotta ends up as a bun. Let it lie in the sieve and place the sieve over a bowl. Let it sit for 24–48 hours in the fridge. You can help the ricotta let go of its liquid by twisting the towel so that it squeezes the cheese. It should release about ³/₈ cup (³/₄ dl) liquid. Throw the liquid out (unless you find some way to use it for another dish).

Butter a spring form and powder with flour (8.5–9 inches diameter). Roll ¾ of the dough out into a round, about 12 inches in diameter and about 3-5 mm thick. Carefully move the dough into the spring form and fold the edges upwards. Cover the bottom with the filling. Fold the edges in over the edges of the filling. If it is very uneven, you may cut the dough evenly over the filling and later fold it down.

Roll out the rest of the dough just as thinly. Cut in shreds 5-10 mm wide and arrange in a plaid pattern over the filling.

Bake in the middle of the oven to a nice color, about 45–55 minutes. Let it cool on a baking grid before you remove the ring. Sprinkle powdered sugar on top and serve.

Torta della nonna
Grandma's torte, Tuscany

This is a torte (a filled cake) that you see all over Italy, from north to south. However, it is believed that it originated in Tuscany.

There are several accepted recipes out there and the debate over which is best can be just as fierce as debates over the best *ragu* (or rather, there really is no debate: one's own grandmother's—or mamma's—is always the best!). Some times ricotta, preferably made with sheep's milk, is added to the filling, but here we've used a lemony fresh vanilla cream, *crema pasticcera*. The dough for the crust, *pasta frolla*, is different from the one used in *cassata al forno*.

Pasta frolla:
6 tbsp (100 g) butter
6 oz (175 g) flour
2 tsp finely grated lemon zest
1/2 tsp vanilla sugar
1 egg
1.7 oz (50 g) sugar

Crema pasticcera:
1 vanilla stick
2 1/2 cups (5 dl) milk
1 large piece of lemon peel
3 egg yolks
3.5 oz (100 g) sugar
1.7 oz (50 g) cornstarch
powdered sugar
3.5 oz (100 g) pine nuts

Pasta frolla: Let the butter reach room temperature. Place butter, flour, grated lemon zest, and powdered vanilla in a bowl and use your hands to work it into crumbly dough.

Add the egg and sugar and mix until smooth. If the dough is too loose add some flour; if it is too firm, add some water.

Shape the dough into a large ball, wrap it in plastic wrap, and let it chill in the fridge for at least half an hour.

Crema pasticcera: Cut the vanilla stick in half lengthwise and scrape out the seeds into a pot. (You may place the rest of the vanilla stick in a jar with sugar to create your own vanilla sugar.) Add milk and a large piece of lemon peel. Carefully heat right up to the boiling point.

Mix egg yolks, sugar, and cornstarch in a large bowl. Whisk in the warm milk a little at the time.

When everything is well blended, pour it back into the pot. Heat it, stirring constantly, until it becomes a thick cream. Remove from the stove. Cover with plastic wrap and place the pot in a cold water bath to cool. When the cream has cooled, prepare the crust.

La torta: Set the oven to 350 F / 175 C degrees. Roll out the pie dough and place in a pie dish with a removable bottom, about 9 inches/ 24 cm in diameter. Prick with a fork.

Remove the lemon peel from the vanilla cream and pour into the pie shell. Smooth out the surface and cover with pine nuts and sift some powdered sugar over the top. Bake in the oven for 25–30 minutes until the crust is a nice golden brown. Serve cool.

Zabaione
Zabaione, Piemont

North meets south in this delicious, egg yolk-based pudding. Although this dessert originated in Piemont, the wine used, Marsala, is Sicilian. Great with fresh fruit and berries.

4 egg yolks
1/2 cup (1 dl) dry marsala wine (or other dry white wine or dry sparkling wine)
1 tbsp vanilla sugar

Whisk the egg yolks in a stainless bowl until frothy. Create a double boiler and continue whisking the eggs over simmering water, adding the wine a little at a time. Whisk until the eggs thicken, being careful not to heat the eggs too much, because they can easily cook and harden. Remove from the double boiler. Flavor with vanilla sugar. Serve warm or cold.

Tiramisù

A dessert you will find at any self-respecting restaurant—and even those without self-respect. Through the years we have tested various recipes and this is the best one we've come across. We make this using an Italian coffee maker, the stove-top aluminum brewer known as a *moka*. You can easily double this recipe to serve a large group of people.

Tiramisu tastes even better when you allow it to rest for a bit. Prepare it the day before and let it rest in the fridge overnight. Give it a few days and it'll be even more delicious. You may either make one large tray and have each guest cut their own piece, or you may make individual portions of tiramisu in some sort of glass.

¾ cup (1 ½ dl) strong coffee, preferably espresso from a moka
1 egg
7 oz (200 g) mascarpone
2 ½ tbsp powdered sugar
1 tbsp rum
1 tbsp cognac
10–12 (½ pack) ladyfingers
Cocoa powder

Brew the coffee and let it cool.

Separate the egg white and the yolk. Whisk mascarpone, powdered sugar, and yolk. Add the 1 tbsp of rum.

Whisk the egg white in a separate bowl until it forms stiff peaks. Fold in the mascarpone mixture.

Blend coffee, cognac, and 1 tbsp rum in a bowl that is large enough for you to dip the ladyfingers in the mixture. Let them absorb the liquid, but not so much that they fall apart.

Arrange the ladyfingers along the bottom of a serving dish or glass. Cover with the mascarpone mix. Add another layer of ladyfingers and cover with the cream. Cover with plastic wrap and place in the fridge overnight. Sprinkle with cocoa powder and serve.

182

Gelato al ganduia
Hazelnut and chocolate ice cream, Piedmont

Gianduia is a blend of hazelnuts and chocolate and is a specialty for Piedmont, where the hazelnut is very popular. They say that the blend was first created in Turin in the mid-1800s. *Gianduia* is made like pralines, chocolate cakes, and Nutella. It is also a very common flavor of ice cream. The name stems from a Piedmont carnival figure and marionette.

In this recipe, the flavor is created from scratch and not through the finished Nutella. It makes a wonderfully creamy ice cream, which is also very filling. It is possible to buy preroasted hazelnuts. Otherwise, roast in the oven or on a dry frying pan and rub the shells off.

4 cups (8 dl) (about 16 oz (450 g)) roasted hazelnuts
4 cups (1 liter) regular milk
6 oz (175 g) dark chocolate of good quality
5 yolks
approximately ½ cup (1 dl) sugar

Save about 50 g (½ cup (1 dl)) hazelnuts. Place the rest of the nuts in a food processor and finely chop.

Warm the milk in a saucepan until you see small bubbles forming along the edges. Remove from the stove and add the chopped hazelnuts. Cool and leave in the fridge overnight.

Sift the hazelnut milk through a fine sieve into a bowl. Squeeze as much of the milk as possible out of the hazelnuts (take some in your hand and squeeze as hard as you can). Throw the nuts away.

Pour the nut milk in a saucepan. Chop the chocolate and add to the milk. Heat while stirring until the chocolate is melted. Remove from the stove.

Whisk yolks and sugar in a large bowl until firm. Stir in the chocolate milk and empty everything back into the saucepan. Carefully simmer while stirring until it thickens to a cream, about 5–8 minutes. Cool in a water bath or in the fridge.

Freeze the cold cream in an ice cream maker by following the directions on the machine, or pour the cream in a plastic container with a lid and place in the freezer. Take out every 30 minutes, stir around, and set back in. Continue until the ice cream is completely frozen. The ice cream will be lighter if you use an ice cream maker.

Chop the remaining hazelnuts and sprinkle on top before serving.

Gelato al cioccolato
Chocolate ice cream, Sicily

This is a typical ice cream of southern Italy, made with milk and no eggs, which makes it lean and feel light and fresh. When you taste the rich, tasty chocolate flavor, it is hard to believe it is made with regular cocoa.

6 oz (175 g) sugar
3 oz (80 g) cocoa
2 tbsp cornstarch
3 ¼ cups (7 ½ dl) regular milk

Blend sugar, cocoa, and cornstarch in a saucepan. Add half of the milk and whisk so that everything dissolves. Warm the blend under constant stirring. Add the rest of the milk after a while. Cool in a water bath or in the fridge.

Freeze the cold cream in an ice cream maker by following the directions on the machine, or pour the cream in a plastic container with a lid and place in the freezer. Take out every 30 minutes, stir around, and set back in. Continue until the ice cream is completely frozen. The ice cream will be lighter if you use an ice cream maker.

Gelato fior di latte
Milk ice cream, Sicily

Fior di latte is almost as popular in Italy as vanilla ice cream is here. The vanilla ice cream is not as common, but then again, it is not uncommon to see Italians flavor the *fior di latte* with vanilla. Use half a vanilla stick, sliced open lengthwise, scrape out the seeds, and let the stick boil with the cream. Remove the vanilla stick before freezing the cream. The original *fior di latte* tasted only of milk and cream—perfect with fresh berries. In this recipe, we also add some apricot marmalade for a fresh taste.

1 ¼ cups (2 ½ dl) heavy whipping cream
3 ¾ cups (7 ½ dl) regular milk
8 oz (225 g) sugar
7 tsp cornstarch
1 tbsp apricot marmalade

Warm cream and 2 ½ cups (5 dl) milk in a saucepan until you see small bubbles appear along the edge (right before it starts boiling). Remove from the stove.

Blend sugar and cornstarch in a bowl. Whisk in 1 ¼ cups (2 ½ dl) milk and stir so that everything dissolves. Stir the cold blend into the hot cream milk. Place the saucepan back on the stove and warm on medium heat while stirring until the cream starts boiling and thickens to a light cream. Stir in the apricot marmalade. Cool in a water bath or in the fridge.

Freeze the cold cream in an ice cream maker by following the directions on the machine, or pour the cream in a plastic container with a lid and place in the freezer. Take out every 30 minutes, stir around, and set back in. Continue until the ice cream is completely frozen. The ice cream will be lighter if you use an ice cream maker.

Gelato al lampone
Raspberry ice cream

Using too many yolks in ice cream results in an eggy taste. To avoid this, we combine egg yolks with cornstarch here to thicken the cream. Some add gelatin for texture and to prevent it from melting quickly, but we feel that real ice cream should contain as little gelatin as possible. Real ice cream *should* melt quickly!

4 yolks
4.4 oz (125 g) sugar
1 cup (2 dl) regular milk
1 ¼ cups (2 ½ dl) cream
0.8 oz (25 g) honey
¼ cup (½ dl) regular milk
1 tbsp cornstarch
1.3 lbs (600 g) raspberries
3.5 oz (100 g) sugar
1 tbsp cornstarch
1.3 lbs (600 g) frozen raspberries
3.5 oz (100 g) sugar

Whisk yolks and sugar until fluffy. Pour 1 cup (2 dl) milk, the cream, and honey in a saucepan and bring to a boil. Whisk the milk mixture into the egg yolk and sugar mixture and blend well. Pour back into the saucepan.

Blend ¼ cup (½ dl) milk and cornstarch and stir in with the ingredients in the saucepan. Heat everything while stirring constantly until it thickens enough to coat the back of a wooden spoon. Cool everything in a water bath.

It is ideal to make the cream in advance. This way, the proteins are allowed to expand properly, which makes for better ice cream. At the very least, let it rest for a few hours before proceeding to the next step.

Thaw the raspberries. Puree with sugar in a food processor. Pass through a sieve to remove the seeds. Blend the raspberry puree with the cream and freeze in an ice cream maker.

Sorbetto al limone
Lemon sorbet

1 ¼ cups (2 ½ dl) fresh-squeezed lemon juice
½ lb (200 g) sugar
0.7 oz (20 g) honey
2 ½ cups (5 dl) water
1 tbsp finely grated lemon zest
1 egg white

Scrub the lemons under running warm water to remove the wax. (In Italy, lemons aren't waxed and therefore the surface is matte. The lemons we buy are waxed so that they will keep better.) Juice the lemons then grate the zest finely, while avoiding the pith.

Heat sugar, honey, and water in a saucepan while stirring until the sugar dissolves. Let the syrup cool. (To speed this process up, you can create a cold water bath in the sink.)

Blend the cold syrup with lemon zest and lemon juice. Freeze in an ice cream maker. When the sorbet starts to freeze and thicken a little, add a lightly whipped egg white to give the sorbet a lighter, fluffier consistency.

Amaretti
Almond cakes

You'll encounter variations on this classic cookie all over Italy. In Sardinia, they are soft and chewy; in Lombardy they are hard. They most likely originated in Sicily, as it was there the Arabs first introduced almonds and sugar to the Italian peninsula.

Amaretti are often served with espresso. They are good crushed with ice cream and fruit salads and are also used as an ingredient in cakes and creams. *Amaretti* don't contain amaretto (an almond-flavored liquer); it is the bitter almond that creates the taste. These cookies are simple to make, but capricious; the result is rarely the same.

About 140:

10 oz (275 g) almonds
1 oz (30 g) bitter almonds
1 lb (500 g) powdered sugar
4 egg whites, medium eggs
granulated sugar

For hard cookies: set the oven to 300 F (150 C) and bake for 20 minutes.
For soft cookies: Set the oven to 390 F (200 C) and bake for 10 minutes.

Weigh almonds and bitter almonds. Scald them, boil for a few minutes, and spoon with cold water so that the shells fall off easily. Dry the almonds and then dry-roast them in a frying pan without allowing them to brown. Let the almonds cool before moving on to the next step.

Grind the almonds into a fine meal in a food processor. Place in a bowl and add the powdered sugar one tablespoon at a time. Whisk egg whites until somewhat fluffy, but not stiff. Combine the egg whites with the almond meal and powdered sugar.

The easiest way to create the cookies is by using an icing piping bag with a large nozzle (or a ziplock bag with one corner cut away) to pipe quarter-sized buttons on parchment paper. Make sure that you leave adequate room between them. Sprinkle some granulated sugar on top. Place in the oven and bake according to desired texture (see above).

Let the cookies cool on the parchment before serving. Store in an airtight container.

Sorbetto all'arancia rossa
Blood orange sorbet, Sicily

Tarocco, sanguinello, and *moro* are the most common blood orange varieties. The red color is the result of a substance the orange develops to protect itself from drastic temperature changes. Blood oranges need cold nights, which they get in Sicily. *Moro* and *tarocco* ripen early in the spring season, whereas *sanguinello* may be harvested as late as April. Moro is the darkest of these and is somewhat bitter. *Tarocco* oranges are sweet and their juice is not as red, but they have the highest vitamin-C content of all oranges. *Sanguinello* are very similar to *moro*.

1 ¼ cups (2 ½ dl) (½ lb (250 g)) water
¾ cup (1 ½ dl) (135 g) sugar
2 ¼ cups (4 ½ dl) (1 lb (450 g)) blood orange juice
the juice of 1 lime

Heat water and sugar while stirring until the sugar dissolves. Let the syrup cool. Juice the oranges. Combine the juice and syrup, then add the lime juice.

Freeze in an ice cream maker. You may serve it immediately or keep in the freezer and serve later. You can also freeze it without an ice cream maker: Pour in a large, covered container and place in the freezer. Take out every 30 minutes to stir and return to the freezer. Repeat until the sorbet has achieved the desired consistency.

Frutta al vino rosso
Fruit boiled in red wine, Valle d'Aosta

Valle d'Aosta is situated in northwest Italy and borders France, Switzerland, and Piedmont. It is one of 5 regions in Italy with a special autonomy (the others are Sardinia, Sicily, Trento-Alto Adige, and Friuli-Venezia Giulia). These regions are autonomous both culturally and linguistically; in Valle d'Aost, for instance, they speak a French-provincial dialect.

For this recipe you may use whatever fruit you like (or whatever you have on hand). Mix multiple kinds of fruit, if desired. Choose firm apples and pears for boiling. Instead of the vanilla stick, you may flavor with cloves and lemon zest.

3 apples
3 pears
1 vanilla stick or 1 clove and ½ lemon, the zest
2 small cinnamon sticks
4 tbsp sugar
2 cups (4 dl) red wine
1 cup (2 dl) sweet marsala, port wine, or other dessert wine
1.5 lb (700 g) plums

Peel the apples and pears. Cut in wedges and remove the cores.

Place in a saucepan. Add the vanilla stick, split down the middle, cinnamon, sugar, red wine, and marsala. Bring to a boil. Let it simmer so that the fruit softens somewhat, about 5–10 minutes.

Cut the plums in half. Add to the saucepan and simmer until soft, about 5 minutes. Be careful not to cook the fruit too long, or it will begin to break apart.

Remove from the stove and let cool, covered. Place in the fridge and let marinate overnight, or for at least 6 hours.

This delicious dessert may be eaten at room temperature or warm. Serve with ice cream or whipped cream and maybe an amaretto cookie (see page 188).

Fragole all'aceto
Strawberries in balsamic vinegar, Emilia–Romagna

If possible, try to get a hold of smaller strawberries or preferably wild strawberries, *fragole selvatica* (wild strawberries) or *del bosco* (from the forest). Not all balsamic vinegar tastes the same; there is a reason why some are more expensive than others. Use a good *aceto balsamico di Modena*.

1 lb (500 g) strawberries or wild strawberries
1–2 tbsp sugar
2 tbsp balsamic vinegar

Rinse the strawberries and remove the tops. Place in a bowl and sprinkle with sugar. Drizzle the balsamic vinegar over the berries and mix carefully.

Cover with plastic wrap and let sit at room temperature for at least 1 hour.

Fragole al vino bianco
Strawberries in white wine, Lazio

This simple and delicious dessert may be flavored with lemon zest for an extra kick. Use a dry white wine, preferably Italian; *frascati* is perfect. It looks especially attractive when the lemon zest is shredded with a zester instead of a regular grater.

1 lb (500 g) strawberries
2–3 tbsp sugar
1 ¼ cups (2 ½ dl) dry white wine
some lemon zest

Rinse the strawberries and remove the tops. Cut into smaller pieces.

Dissolve the sugar in the wine. The amount of sugar depends on how sweet the berries are. Flavor with shredded or grated lemon zest, but avoid using too much as the lemon may overpower the other flavors.

Add the strawberries, stir, cover with plastic wrap, and let marinate for at least 1 hour.

Fragole al vino rosso
Strawberries or wild strawberries in red wine, Tuscany

Small strawberries or wild strawberries are the best. In Tuscany they use red wine from Chianti.

1 lb (500 g) strawberries or wild strawberries
about ½ cup (½ cup (1 dl)) sugar
1 ¼ cups (2 ½ dl) red wine
some lemon zest

Rinse the strawberries and remove the tops. If they are larger, cut them into smaller pieces.

Dissolve the sugar in the wine. Add the strawberries and stir. Cover with plastic wrap, place in the fridge, and let marinate, preferably overnight.

Strain the mixture, setting the strawberries aside and placing the liquid in a saucepan. Add a piece of lemon zest without the pith. Don't use too much as the lemon flavor will overpower the other flavors. Let simmer until the marinade has thickened.

Add more of the lemon zest and let cool.

Arrange the strawberries in serving bowls and pour the wine sauce on top.

Coppa di mascarpone alle pesche

Mascarpone with peaches

A simple and fresh dessert for the adults. It is very important that the fruit be ripe and sweet. You may enhance the flavors with some sugar.

3 ripe peaches or nectarines
5 ½ tbsp amaretto liqueur, orange liqueur, or rum
1 tbsp lemon juice
½ lb (250 g) mascarpone
⅔ cup (¾ dl) (2 oz (60 g)) sugar
1 ¼ cups (2 ½ dl) whipping cream
4–5 cups (8–10 dl) amaretti cookies
2 tbsp roasted almond flakes

Cut the peaches or nectarines in half and remove the pits. Slice or cut into thin wedges. Mix liqueur and freshly squeezed lemon juice in a bowl and set aside.

Whisk mascarpone and sugar in a bowl until fluffy. Whisk the cream until it thickens. Carefully fold the whipped cream into the mascarpone with a silicone spatula. Place the blend at the bottom of a serving glass. Add the fruit. Sprinkle crushed ameretti on top then add a layer of mascarpone cream. Cover with plastic wrap and cool. Sprinkle almonds on top before serving.

Crema di ricotta alla frutta fresca

Fresh fruit with ricotta, Sicily

This is the same cream you use to stuff *cannoli*, the fried pipes you find all over Italy. It is simply a sweet-ened ricotta that is whipped to make a light and fresh alternative to whipped cream. In Sicily, they prefer to use completely fresh ricotta, and preferably sheep's milk ricotta, which has a stronger taste. The fruit varies according to preference and availability, but it has to be ripe, flavorful, and sweet.

6 peaches, nectarines, or apricots
2 cups (½ liter) strawberries
4.4 oz (125 g) raspberries or currants
2 tbsp limoncello or other lemon liqueur

2 tbsp sugar
1 lb (500 g) ricotta
½ tsp grated lemon zest
1 tsp vanilla sugar
¼ cup (½ dl) (1 oz (30 g)) powdered sugar
1 pinch ground cinnamon
dark chocolate

Dice or slice the stone fruits. Cut up the strawberries. Carefully blend with raspberries or currants, liqueur, and sugar in a bowl.

Whisk the ricotta until creamy. Clean the lemon in warm water, dry, and finely grate the peel, avoiding the pith. Mix lemon zest, vanilla sugar, powdered sugar, and cinnamon with the ricotta.

Arrange fruit and berries in serving glasses. Top with the ricotta. Grate chocolate over the cream and serve.

Alexandra Zazzi

RAPALLO, IN LIGURIA, HOLDS A SPECIAL place in Zazzi's heart.

"When I was two and a half years old, we moved to Italy," she tells us. "My childhood was spent in Rapallo."

Alexandra's father's family is from Borgo Val di Taro, in western Emilia–Romagna, but he was born in Berlin and grew up in Söder in Stockholm.

"My grandfather worked at the Italian embassy in Berlin. During the Second World War, he helped Italian Jews get passports that didn't say that they were Jewish so that they could leave Germany. The Germans found out, and my grandfather was sent to "Siberia," which, in this case, was the Italian embassy in Stockholm.

Alexandra's father, Gianfranco met a nurse, Eva; they made a family and a scholarship brought them to Italy later.

"In Rapallo we were *gli svedesi*, the Swedes," Alexandra says. "We were exciting. The Italians are really a very curious people. And if you have even a drop of Italian blood, then you are Italian as well. My mother would make potato dumplings, and they called them gnocchi."

WHEN THE OIL CRISIS HIT IN THE 1970s, the job disappeared and the family moved back to Sweden.

"In Sweden, we didn't fit in. It took a long time before I felt Swedish."

Food is an important tie to her Italian heritage.

"As an Italian you are a natural food lover," she states. "All Italians are amateur chefs, for better or worse. And everyone thinks they know best."

Alexandra entered the restaurant business through a summer job as a 15-year-old at a hamburger chain. And it continued from there.

Alexandra Zizzi has run two restaurants and is now working with catering, events, and as a food critic. What's more, she's a winner of the Swedish edition of the reality show *Survivor*.

"There is a pride and nostalgia in Italian food. And a homemade meal can be better than anything else. It is a given that you'll cook with the right ingredients, ingredients that are from the region and in season. You can't go wrong."

Profiterole al cioccolato
Petits choux with chocolate sauce

Profiterole or *bignè* is the Italian equivalent to the French *beignet* or *petits choux*. "They're so delicious that you shiver with pleasure," Alexandra says. "Serve with a mix of sweet and somewhat tart berries. I usually arrange all of the *profiterole* on a plate and then pour the chocolate sauce on top of the deliciousness."

Profiterole, about 20:
1 ¼ cups (2 ½ dl) water
½ tsp salt
⅓ cup (100 g) butter
1 tbsp granulated sugar
1 ¼ cups (2 ½ dl) wheat flour
1 tsp vanilla sugar
3 medium eggs

Filling:
1 vanilla stick
¼ cup (½ dl) milk
3 tbsp sugar
1 tbsp wheat flour
1 tbsp potato flour
3 yolks
1 ¼ cups (2 ½ dl) hard whipped cream
1 tbsp grated orange zest, preferably from an organic orange
1 tbsp Cointreau

Chocolate sauce:
1 ¼ cups (2 ½ dl) whipping cream
5 oz (150 g) dark chocolate, 70% cacao content

Profiterole: Set the oven to 390 F (200 C). Bring water to a boil with salt, butter, and sugar. Add the flour a little at a time while stirring with a wooden spoon. Continue heating the blend on low heat until the batter no longer sticks to the walls of the saucepan or the spoon. Remove from the heat, add vanilla sugar, and carefully stir in the eggs, one at a time. Let it cool somewhat then scoop small balls onto a buttered baking sheet. Remember that they will double in size.

Bake in the oven until they are golden, about 12-14 minutes. Remove from the oven and let cool.

Filling: Cut the vanilla stick in half lengthwise and scape out the seeds. Heat the milk until just lukewarm then stir in the sugar, vanilla seeds and stick, wheat flour, and potato flour. Whisk in egg yolks one at a time. Simmer gently, stirring for a few minutes, until the mixture thickens. Remove the vanilla stick. When the mixture has cooled, fold in the whipped cream, liqueur, and orange peel. Pipe the filling into the profiterole.

Chocolate sauce: Melt chocolate in a double boiler. Heat the cream in a saucepan and stir in the chocolate. Pour the chocolate sauce over the profiterole and serve immediately.

Fichi al forno
Oven-baked figs, Sicily

The fig is an ancient Mediterranean fruit that grows uncultivated. The fruits are sensitive to impact, and they go bad quickly after being harvested. When they are ripe, you can see a little golden drop of nectar peeking out. Fig trees can withstand Swedish and American winters and they bear a lot of fruit.

For this dessert, which is made with Middle Eastern spices, you should be just fine with imported figs, but in other cases only the ripe, newly harvested figs will do.

12 figs
the juice of 2 oranges
¾ cup (1 ½ dl) red wine
2 cloves
1 cinnamon stick
nutmeg
honey
roasted almonds or pomegranate seeds

Set the oven to 440 F (225 C). Make two slits at the top of each fig as if you were cutting them into quarters, but don't cut more than a slit. Place them on a baking sheet.

Blend orange juice, red wine, cloves, cinnamon stick, some grated nutmeg, and honey in a saucepan. The amount of honey depends on the sweetness of the oranges. Let it carefully boil down to about half the volume. Pour the sauce over the figs and bake in the oven for about 10 minutes. Let cool. Sprinkle roasted almonds or pomegranate seeds on top before serving.

Panna cotta
Cream pudding, Piedmont

This is the authentic panna cotta, which is simply cooked cream with minimal flavors added—just some lemon zest. Now that panna cotta is served with all kinds of flavors, it seems exciting to go back to the original. It is often served this way in Rome and always with fresh berries—strawberries, raspberries, wild strawberries, red or black currants, or a mix with some of each.

You can make a basic sauce by passing berries through a sieve and then sweetening with powdered sugar as needed. Save a few berries for a garnish. You arrive at the most classic flavor by allowing half a vanilla stick to boil with the cream and milk mixture. Then let it cook for a while before you continue with the recipe.

2 gelatin sheets or 1 tsp gelatin powder
2 ½ whipping cream
¼ cup (½ dl) regular milk
1.7 oz (50 g) (about ½ dl) sugar

¼–½ lemon, zest
about ½ lb (250 g) (2 ½ cups (5 dl)) berries
about 1 tbsp powdered sugar
mint leaves

Soak gelatin sheets in cold water for 10 minutes. Squeeze to remove excess water. If you use gelatin powder, let it soak in
1 tbsp cold water for 5 minutes.

Bring cream, milk, sugar, and lemon zest to a boil. Simmer for 1 minute. Pass through a sieve to remove the lemon zest.

Add the gelatin and stir so that it dissolves. Pour into portion-sized baking cups, preferably metal cups as they are easier to handle. Let them chill in the fridge for 4 hours until they are firm.

Run a spoon under warm water, then carefully slide it along the inside of the cups; the pudding will come loose easily. Flip out onto plates, garnish with fruit and/or sauce and mint leaf.

Cantuccini
Almond biscotti, Tuscany

Also called *biscotti di Prato* after the city in northern Tuscany. Today there are so many variations and interpretations of this beloved cookie that it feels exotic to return to the original. If you still wish for some variation, you can add ½ lb (200 g) chopped chocolate. As another alternative, the orange zest may be replaced with lemon zest. These are crunchy cookies that make a nice addition to desserts when crushed, and are particularly good as a topping for whipped cream and fruit.

About 2 plates:

½ lb (250 g) sugar
1 tbsp vanilla sugar
3 eggs
1 orange, zest
½ lb (200 g) almonds
14 oz (400 g) wheat flour
1 tsp baking powder
pinch salt

Set the oven to 350 F (175 C). Whisk sugar, vanilla sugar, and eggs until fluffy and light.

Wash the orange in warm water, dry it off, and grate the zest, avoiding the pith. Add to the egg mixture along with the whole almonds. Blend flour, baking powder, and salt in a separate bowl and sift it into the egg mixture. Work into dough. Add more flour if it is too sticky—but the dough should be quite sticky. Shape into a log and cover with plastic wrap or aluminum foil. Let it sit in the fridge for at least 30 minutes.

Shape into logs about 2 fingers thick. Place on a baking sheet lined with parchment paper. Flatten the dough somewhat. Bake for about 35 minutes, or until it turns light brown. Remove from the oven and slice diagonally into ⅓ inch (1 ¼ cm) thick cookies. Cool. Store in an airtight container so that they stay crisp.

Biscotti brutti ma buoni
Hazelnut cookies, Piedmont

"Ugly but tasty," a fitting name. Here they are made with hazelnuts, but you can also make these with almonds. If you wish, you can add ½ tsp ground cinnamon for added flavor.

14 oz (400 g) roasted and peeled hazelnuts
6 egg whites
31 oz (30 g) sugar
1 tbsp vanilla sugar

Preheat the oven to 350 F (175 C).

You can usually buy roasted and peeled hazelnuts. If you can't find them, you can dry-roast them in a frying pan and rub the skins off with your fingers or a kitchen towel. Finely grind the hazelnuts in a food processor.

Whisk egg whites until stiff in a bowl. Blend sugar and vanilla sugar in a separate bowl. Fold the ground hazelnuts into the egg white foam. Then fold in the sugar, a little at a time.

Pour the mixture in a large nonstick frying pan. Heat over low heat, stirring constantly with a wooden spoon until the blend thickens, about 20 minutes. It should be hard to stir.

Scoop tablespoon-sized balls onto parchment paper. Do not arrange them too close together. Bake until golden, about 15–20 minutes. Let cool on the parchment paper.

Baci

Kisses, Veneto

Baci di dama, lady kisses, or *baci di Giulietta* as they are called in Verona, after the heroine of Shakespeare's *Romeo and Juliet*, which is set there.

1 cup (250 g) butter
2 oz (60 g) powdered sugar
1 tbsp rum
11 oz (315 g) flour
3.5 oz (100 g) dark chocolate
2 tbsp butter

Let the butter reach room temperature. Stir butter and powdered sugar until fluffy. Add rum. Stir in flour and mix until well blended. Cover with plastic wrap and let it rest for 1 hour in the fridge.

Preheat the oven to 350 F (175 C). Shape the dough into small balls of about 1 teaspoon each. Place them about 1 inch (a couple of centimeters) apart on a lined baking sheet. Bake until they are hard and golden, about 15 minutes. Cool on a baking grid.

Heat chocolate and butter in a double boiler while stirring until it melts and blends nicely. As an alternative, you can melt it in the microwave. Heat in many shorter segments so that you don't burn the chocolate, removing it from the microwave and stirring in between.

Spread some of the melted chocolate on the flat bottom of one cookie. Stick it to a second cookie. Repeat until there are none left.

Valle d'Aosta

Lombardy

Trentino-
Alto Adige

Friuli-
Venezia
Guilia

● Torino

● Milano

Venezia ●

Veneto

Piedmont

Emilia-Romagna

Liguria

● Genova

● Bologna

● Firenze

Tuscany

Marche

Umbria

Lazio

Abruzzo

● Roma

Molise

Sardegna

Campania

Basilicata

Puglia

● Napoli

Calabria

● Palermo

Sicilia

204

LE REGIONI
the regions

ON MARCH 17, 1861, ITALY WAS UNITED as one kingdom, *la Repubblica Italiana*. But *Italy* as a term was common long before then, even if the root of it is unclear. At first, *Italy* only referred to the southern part of the peninsula, the area the Greeks colonized during the 800s and 900s BC. During the Roman era, the name started to encompass the whole peninsula. Different territories within Italy have been controlled by different powers over the course of history. When the Greeks colonized the southern part of the peninsula, they called it *Magna Graecia*. The Etruscans dominated for a while and were replaced by the Romans. The South of Italy has been ruled by practically every power that has ever dominated the Mediterranean Sea.

Before unification, Italy was made up of small states, city states, and kingdoms. The hilly landscape separated the regions, and they differed in language, culture—and food.

During the 1300s, Dante Alighieri devoted himself to creating a common language for Italy, a blend of his own Tuscan and Sicilian. However, when Italy was finally unified in 1861, very few Italians understood or spoke Italian. It was not until the 1960s that the majority of Italians knew the language well.

In 1992, the EU did an inventory and found that there were 13 distinct spoken languages in Italy. Furthermore, there was an equal number of dialects that were just as distinct from Italian as they were from Latin. Many of these languages and dialects are still very much alive. On Wikipedia you can, for instance, find pages in Napolitano, Sardinian, Sicilian, Venetian, and Emiliano–Romagnolo. Friulian, Ligurian, Genovese, Lombardese, Piedmontese, Greek, and Albanian are also all spoken in Italy. But this is slowing changing in favor of Italian. TV has had a large influence in this.

WHEN LANGUAGES AND CULTURES MERGE cuisines merge as well. When southern Italians moved north during the 1950s and '60s to work in factories, they would bring dried pasta with them. Thirty years ago, one would eat *panettone* in Milan and *pandoro* in Turin; now you find both of these cakes all over Italy. Thanks to industrialization and television commercials, foods that were once only produced and consumed in certain regions are now popular all over the country.

In spite of this, the sense of local and regional identity is still very strong. One dish or other may be a hit all over the country, but northern Italians will always prefer their own cuisine over that of the South. And the other way around.

TALKING ABOUT ONE ITALIAN CUISINE IS UNTHINKABLE. If you say "Italian food," you are referring to multiple food cultures. The Romans eat Roman food; Tuscans eats Tuscan food. It's not difficult to understand that the cuisine of the Tyrolean Alps is different from that of Sicily, which is closer to Africa than Rome. Eighty miles separate Bologna and Florence, and there are just over 170 miles between Florence and Rome, but the cuisine, culture, and identity differ greatly.

Not many foreign influences have really been integrated into Italian culture. Only a few years ago, there was a note in a Roman paper that a restaurant was opening with foreign food—and it was a *Neapolitan* restaurant. The distance between Rome and Naples is all of 125 miles.

When you're abroad, you might be Italian. But in Italy, you are Venetian, Roman, Neapolitan.

This sometimes extreme local patriotism is called *campanilismo*, after *campanile*, clock tower. The same way you would protect your clock tower against intruders, you protect your local food culture. This applies not only to regions but also to cities, towns, relatives, and families. Every family will protect its recipe for ragù, so that it can pass unchanged from one generation to the next.

Italia nord—northern Italy

Valle d'Aosta—The smallest region borders France, Switzerland, and Piedmont. It is one of five states with a special autonomy. The others are Trentino–Alto Adige and Friuli–Venezia Giulia in the north and Sardinia and Sicily in the south. This means that they, to varying extents, get to keep their taxes within the region (from 60% in Friuli–Venezia Giulia to 100% in Sicily) in exchange for the responsibility of paying for their own schools, health care, and most infrastructure.

The regions are also autonomous when it comes to language and culture. After the Second World War, people were afraid that many would emigrate out of Italy to the countries their regions bordered. In Valle d'Aosta, they speak a dialect based on Provençal, a dialect of France.
Typical foods: cheeses like fontina and robiola, fondue.

Piedmont—The name means "at the foot of the mountain." Turin was the capital of the Kingdom of the Two Sicilies and later of the kingdom of Italy (1849–1861). There are many French influences. Slow food was first created by a Piedmontese man, Carlo Petrini.
Typical foods: vitello tonnato, bagna caoda, grissini, risotto, salsa verde, zabaione.

Liguria—With its sailing heritage, a region that has given us Christopher Columbus and the Genoa sail. Genoa was one of the four rich and powerful maritime republics. The others were Venice, Amalfi, and Pisa.
Typical foods: focaccia, pesto alla Genovese.

Lombardy—Was dominated by the Spaniards for 200 years. Risotto with saffron reflects this part of the region's history. The Austrian period left the Milanese variety of weiner schnitzel. Also known for lots of cheese and charcuteries.
Typical foods: mostarda, polenta, ossobuco, mascarpone, bresaola, panettone, torrone.

Trentino–Alto Adige—Alto Adige is also called Sudtirol. It feels Austrian, and people speak German. Trentino is more Italian. Large, prolific apple orchards resemble vineyards.
Typical foods: gnocchi, speck, strudel.

Veneto—Verona, Vicenza, and Venice. Venetian cuisine is characterized foremost by fish and shellfish fresh from the lagoon or dried as *baccalà*. The spices used are the result of trade with the eastern Mediterranean Sea and Asia. A glass of wine in the afternoon, *l'ombra*, with a few bite-sized snacks is very popular. The rest of Veneto is fertile farmland. *Pandoro* is from Verona.
Typical foods: squid ink black risotto, black pasta, sarde in saor, risi e bisi, radicchio, tiramisù.

Friuli–Venezia Giulia—Note that this region does not include Venezia, Venice. Here you find a blend of old Roman roots, the superpower Austria–Hungary, and Slavic influences. Friuli–Venezia Giulia was formed as late as 1947; the capital, Trieste, was included in 1954. The region produces (and cooks with) a lot of corn.
Typical foods: polenta, cevapcici, San Daniele ham.

Emilia–Romagna—Healthy, rich, food-loving, the stomach of Italy. Bologna, *La Grassa*, the fat one (like mortadella, which orignated there) is the city everyone most associates with food. Parma has both ham and cheese. Fine charcuterie. With Campania and Puglia, this region is also the largest producer of tomatoes, beans, and peas.

Typical foods: fresh and dried egg pasta, lasagna, cannelloni, balsamic vinegar, ravioli.

Italia central, centro —
central Italy

Marche—The Japan of Italy, where everything is manufactured. Even the food seems manufactured; you often stuff one thing into another.

Typical foods: vincisgraddi (lasagna), porchetta.

Tuscany—Here you find a lot of culture, many historical places—Florence, Siena, Volterra, Pisa—and a local patriotism close to the extreme. The food is clearly rustic and rooted in poorer times. Just like in Rome, they eat cow stomach, *trippa*. Tuscans are known as *mangia fagioli*, bean

eaters. Olive oil and charcuteries reign. Typical foods: acquacotta (a thick, rich soup), bistecca alla fiorentina (grilled T-bone), panforte (spice cake), ribollita (soup with bread), pappardelle.

Umbria— Known as *Terra Santa*, holy ground, since four of the most popular saints are from Umbria. Black truffle, and some white. So much charcuterie that *norceria* (after the city Norcia) is synonymous with charcuterie and a *norcino* is a pork butcher.

Typical foods: porchetta, handmade pasta, Baci chocolate from Perugia.

Lazio—Dominated by Rome, which has always been a tourist attraction. All roads lead to Rome, whether religious, political, or touristic. Yet, the city still feels almost small when you're sitting at a trattoria. Rome is a city whose inhabitants have always eaten often at restaurants because one lives in such tight quarters. The food is simple—more like Naples than Bologna. *Il quinto quarto*, the fifth fourth (intestines), are popular.

Typical foods: simple pasta dishes, Jerusalem artichokes, suppli, saltimbocca.

Italia Meridionale, Mezzogiorno—Southern Italy

Abruzzo—The Apennines' roof rises up to 9,800 feet (3,000 meters) and unfortunately stands at risk of an earthquake. Here they love chili pepper, *peperoncino*, and goats strut about. Makes good dry industrial pasta.
Typical foods: Barges carrying charcoal paved the way for pasta alla carbonara, which made its way to Rome.

Molise—The second smallest of all the regions. Up until 1963, it was part of a region with Abruzzo, *Abruzzi e Molise*. *Peperoncino* is very popular and has many names: *diavolicchio, diavolillo, pepento, cazzariello, saitti och lazzariello.* Sheep, pork, and cheeses. Along the coast, fish.
Typical foods: porchetta, maccheroni alla chitarra, scamorza (cheese).

Puglia—Just like Sicily, Puglia was the granary of the Roman Empire.
Today, Puglia is Italy's granary, *il granaio d'Italia.* Here they cultivate lots of olives, wheat, tomatoes, grapes, Jerusalem artichokes, and all kinds of vegetables. They grow large and they grow quickly. The Greek and Arabic heritage is clearly noticeable. Vegetables, fish and shellfish, and pasta. Raw foods, for instance, fish, are a specialty.
Typical foods: taralli (small crackers shaped like rings), calzone.

Campania—The Greeks founded Naples, which has become the center of southern Italy. Many rulers have taken Campania, but few have left traces of their own cuisines. Naples and Campania have created most on their own: pizza, pasta, tomato sauce, and mozzarella. This is a blessedly beautiful and fertile region with a perfect climate for produce. *Campania felix* the Romans would say—happy Campania.
Typical foods: insalata caprese, limoncello, dried pasta, pastries.

Basilicata—A little hidden and sometimes forgotten, but because it is situated in the South, a depository of influences left by foreign powers over the years. *Cucina povera*, poor cuisine, dominates. Bell peppers and *peperoncino*.
Typical foods: penne all'arrabbiata.

Calabria—A toe that almost touches Sicily. Every conqueror of the Mediterranean has been here and left behind traces of their culture in the food and language. Unlike the rest of Italy, the tradition here is to eat a real breakfast, more like a lunch, and preferably at a trattoria. Together with Sicily and Puglia, Calabria was part of *Magna Graecia*, and the Greeks founded many of their cities. Fish, bell peppers, eggplant, and citrus (the last two thanks to the Arabs).
Typical foods: parmigiana di melanzane, pitta (pizza), 'nduja (sausage).

Le Isole—the islands

Sardegna—The next-to-largest island in the Mediterranean Sea, counted as part of southern Italy mostly for historical reasons. Here they produce pecorino, both their own and the Roman kind. There are also a lot of sheep as well as most of Italy's *bottarga*, dried fish roe. Before, people would live in the inlands and not along the coasts because of a fear of intruders. The conquerors stopped by here as well. Fish and shellfish are very much appreciated nowadays, especially crawfish. The Spanish heritage is obvious in both the food and language around Alghero.
Typical foods: pane carasau, malloreddus-pasta.

Sicilia—The largest island in the Mediterranean really is an impressive size. The Greeks were early to found colonies, and they thought the island was the birthplace of gastronomy. Fertile, ideal climate with lots of water. Every conqueror has been here. The Greeks brought wheat, cheese, and wine. The Arab influence is the most obvious. The Arabs brought, among other things, almonds, citrus, apricots, melons, saffron, spices, eggplant, and sugar. They also came with sweets and ice cream. The Spaniards brought cocoa, tomatoes, and corn.
Typical foods: caponata, cassata, arancini, marzipan, ice cream, and sorbet.

OLIO DI OLIVA *olive oil*

OLIVE TREES CAN BE SEEN ALL OVER ITALY, from the North to Sicily in the South.

It takes about 11 pounds (5 kilos) of olives to make four cups (1 liter) of olive oil.

Olives are harvested in November, December, and January.

Extra vergine means that the olives are cold-pressed, so that the solid parts, *sansa*, and water, *acqua*, are separated from the oil. In the making of cheaper oils, the olives are heated so that they release more oil. In making even cheaper oils, chemicals are used to extract the maximum amount of oil. If the label only says olive oil, it means that it is a blend of chemically extracted oils and *extra vergine*.

Many distributors of well-known olive brands don't guarantee more than that the oil is *extra vergine* and that it is made in Italy. *Extra Vergine* should be printed with large letters, and then in smaller letters it should

say that it is produced in Italy. The labels may give the impression that there are Italian olives in the oil, but most often they are from Spain, Greece, Turkey, or North Africa

Italy produces five times more olive oil than what its olive crops allow. In other words, they import a lot of olives. This doesn't mean that these oils are bad; they might just not be as good as one might think. Try a few and find an oil you like. Olive oil is not too expensive and can be used as an everyday oil in cooking.

IF YOU PREFER HIGH-QUALITY OIL, checking that it is *extra vergine* is not enough. In that case, you should also check the origin, so that you know where the olives are from and that they have most likely been pressed a very short time after harvesting. The second olives are picked from the tree, a little wound appears where acid may form. Acid is the worst enemy of olives because it

Carli Fratelli

allows oxidation to begin, which causes decay. Therefore, it is better that the olives be picked carefully by hand than by machine.

The longer the time between when the olives are picked and when they are pressed, the worse the oil ends up. This affects the flavor, and it can also mean that the healthy qualities of the oil are lost. You will usually be able to find information about the oil's place of origin on the back label. There should be a unique number for each bottle. Olive oil is in many ways like wine—there are cheap blends, and then there are finer varieties from established orchards.

These oils will naturally be more expensive. Buy multiple kinds with different flavor characteristics. They are mostly used raw as a dressing over vegetables and salads or as a finishing touch to a prepared dish. In other words, one bottle lasts for a long time.

There's a whole world of exciting oils to discover. Peppery, fatty, watery . . . Many are tasty enough that you can pour the oil on a plate and soak it up with bread, and that will be enough (which, by the way, makes a very good breakfast).

Olive oil doesn't like being heated too much. Partly because the oil can't handle it—it destroys the nutrients—and partly because it won't taste as good. For high-temperature cooking or frying, Italians will mostly use sunflower oil, which can handle more heat. Do not store your olive oil in the fridge. It won't taste bad or be ruined, but all of the changes in temperature mean that it will not last as long. In other words, if you keep oil in the fridge, its shelf life will be shorter. The oil is just fine at room temperature, preferably in a cool and dark place. It definitely shouldn't be placed above the oven (which spices don't like either, by the way).

THE CHARACTER OF OLIVE OIL VARIES from region to region, and it also depends on what kind of olives are used. You can say that oils from Liguria are often mild and finely tuned; the Tuscan oils are more intense, fruity, and sometimes also peppery; Sicilian oils are peppery; and oils from Puglia (which produces almost 40% of all olive oil) are stronger and even more peppery. The color of oils varies, but it might not always speak to the flavor.

The first press after the olives are harvested is called *novello*. It is cloudier and has a rawer taste. It has a different character than stored oil and can be fantastically good. The oil that's not consumed as *novello* will be stored in rust-free barrels. During this stage, the cloudy bits of sediment sink to the bottom and you are left with a clearer oil with a more mature taste. The oil may also be filtered.

Extra vergine is a quality grade based on the acid content. Low acid content is better. Low acid means that the breakdown of the healthy nutrients has not yet begun. An *extra vergine* cannot have acid content of more than 0.8%. The very best oils will have about 0.1%.

VINO *wine*

THE GREEKS BROUGHT WINE to the Italian peninsula. It was the beginning of a beautiful friendship.

Italy and France are the world's biggest wine producers and usually trade the honor of being number one back and forth between them. In 2009, France was the biggest; the year before, it was Italy. (Spain and the United States then follow.) Spain has the largest wine territories, followed by France and Italy. When it comes to consumption, Italy is third, despite the fact that wine drinking has gone down 50% in the last thirty years. (France is number 1 and the Unites States number 2.)

But in many ways, Italy is a country in which things happen on a small scale. Italian industry is composed of many small businesses and very few larger ones. The landscape is made up of small towns and cities, which in turn belong to the small provinces that form the 20 regions. Italy became one united country as late as 1861 (at least on paper). This jumbled-up puzzle is mirrored in the country's winemaking tradition as well. There are 810,000 registered winemakers. Italy cultivates more than 1,000 different kinds of grapes, out of which 350 varieties are Italian grapes. In other words, there is a large spectrum, just as there is with Italian food.

Over the last 40 years, the wine industry in Italy has undergone significant changes. Yes, Italy accounts for a large portion of world production, but the reputation of Italian wine has not always been the best. For many years, Italian wine was better known for the pretty bottles it came in, which were used as candle holders in Italian restaurants around the world, than it was for being good. Time and again, scandals came to light that showed that they tampered with the wines and mixed in things that had no business being there.

Improvement came when the methods and techniques that had brought success in the United States and Australia were applied in Italy. Italian winemakers pulled themselves together, modernized, acquired stainless steel tanks, and streamlined production. New producers have emerged; old wine regions have been given new life. The proportion of bland table wines has declined from almost 90% of production in the 1980s to just over 40%. The general level of quality has gone up, and Italians now produce wines of the highest quality.

Which wine should you choose with your food? One way to begin is to look at the region the wine is from. Often this is the way it is in Italy, because one preferably eats and drink locally. Often, this is a very good choice, since both food and drink are grown in the same ground—the flavors fit together. In Italy, it is, in most cases, practically impossible to do otherwise, because the supply of wines from other regions is small in stores.

Four-fifths of Italy is hilly or mountainous, and most of the country is suitable for wine production. Farthest north, the Alps protect vineyards from cold northern winds. And along the entire peninsula runs the Apennines mountain range, which absorbs heat before it can hit the middle and South. The result is it is possible to produce wine in all 20 regions.

THERE ARE FOUR DIFFERENT TYPES OF WINE IN ITALY:

Vino da Tavola, VdT, table wine

These wines are the bottom and don't have to pass many criteria other than names and color. But that does not mean that all of these wines are bad. Some wineries do not care about labels or do not adhere to the criteria of, for example, using only a certain variety of grapes. This is becoming increasingly common in Italy.

Indicazione Geografica Tipica, IGT

These wines must come from a certain area and include grapes typical of that location. Many talented and serious winemakers make wines in this class, which may compete with the very best.

Denominazione di Origine Controllata, DOC

Rules and Regulations were introduced as late as the 1960s, after the French model for improving and assuring quality. The areas are well defined for varieties and grape blends, and everything is designed to protect local traditions. The rules are different for different regions and wines.

Denominazione di Origine Controllata e Garantita, DOCG

These wines came in existence in an effort to be a bit stricter and ensure even better wines. Among other things, the wines are tasted before approval, much like Parmesan cheese before it is stamped with the brand.

Examples of the label not being everything in Italy are the so-called Super Tuscans, which appeared in the late 1960s. The white grapes that a wine like *chianti classico* should contain were replaced with cabernet sauvignon and merlot. This wine was disqualified for DOC and DOCG. But the wine was far from wines put into plastic containers at the grocery store. They became very popular, and were closely followed in popularity by the prestigious winehouse Antinori, which had made wine for more than 600 years. New wine regions where wines had not been produced previously and new grapes and blends have since then followed. IGT appeared after Super Tuscans.

Wine regions:

Valle d'Aosta—The smallest region with small farms and limited production. Own grapes.

Piedmont—Strong tradition, many of own grapes. The seventh largest wine in Italy, but has the most DOC and DOCG areas. Wines: Barolo, Barbaresco, Asti.

Liguria—Second-smallest producer, but still grows a variety of grapes.

Lombardy—The largest consumer with Milan, but only medium-sized producer. Wines: sparkling Franciacorta, considered the best in Italy, Valtellina.

Trentino-Alto Adige—The northernmost region with a very effective wine production, sometimes on their own grapes. Wines: Alto Adige, Trentino.

Veneto—The largest wine producer in Italy. Even the greatest producer of the DOC and DOCG. Wines: Soave, Valpolicella, Amarone from Verona, Brescia, Prosecco.

Friuli-Venezia Giulia—Known since the 1970s for its white wines.

Emilia-Romagna—The region is so famous and acclaimed for their food, but on a smaller scale as winemaker. This is not due to amount, because they are second only to the Veneto of the northern producers, but due to quality. Wines: light bubbly lambrusco, red, white, or rosé.

Marche—Produces a lot of white wine. The red seldom reaches outside the region. Wine: Verdicchio.

Tuscany—From straw bottles and diluting scandals to respected wine. The eighth largest producer measured in quantity, third behind Veneto and Piedmont in the production of the classified wines. Maremma has emerged as a new wine producer. Wines: Chianti classico, Brunello di Montalcino, Vernaccia di San Gimignano, Vino Nobile di Montepulciano, wine santo.

Umbria—Their Orvieto is one of Italy's most exported white wines. Also produces typical wines of central Italy and grow some of its own grapes.

Lazio—Romans love the easily consumed white wine that is produced in large amounts. But the red that they make little of gets the best reviews. Wines: Frascati, Est! est! est! di Montefiascone.

Abruzzo—Known for its red Montepulciano d'Abruzzo, not to be confused with Tuscany's Vino Nobile di Montepulciano. Fifth place in terms of

production quantity. Wine: The white Trebbiano d'Abruzzo.

Molise—One of the smallest within production. Two DOCs. Wines: Biferno, Molise.

Puglia—The heel, where the hot climate gives the wine too high alcohol percentages. Moving from merely producing great quantities, they now also make good wine. Grapes are negro amaro, Primitivo (which became the zinfandel in California) and malvasia nera. Wines: Copertino, Salice Salentino.

Campania—The Greeks brought grapes like Greco, Falanghina, and Aglianico. Romans also cultured wine here. The old Roman and Greek grapes are still grown; several grapes specific to the region have been rediscovered, and they now make wine of great quality. Wines: Fiano di Avellino, Greco di Tufo, Aglianico Taburno, Vesuvio.

Basilicata—The region of the "arch." Small wineries.

Wine: Aglianico del Vulture with original Greek grapes is considered one of Italy's foremost wines.

Calabria—The Greeks were especially fond of cultivating wine here. Local grapes: gaglioppo and greco. Wines: Cirò, Greco di Bianco

Sardinia—Ruling people have come and gone on the island—Phoenicians, Carthaginians, Romans, and Spaniards. The grapes remain and have recently gained popularity. Wines: Cannonau di Sardegna, Monica di Sardegna, Vermentino and Nuragus.

Sicily—The largest island in the Mediterranean has not only been a major producer of grain, vegetables, and fruit, but also of wine. More volume than quality, but the change has begun. Great potential and above all, attracts Etna's volcanic soils. The rulers have left their grapes. Inzolia, nero d'avola, nerello mascalese, Carricante, and Grillo are some of the local grapes. Wines: strong wine Marsala, Cerasuolo di Vittoria.

ALTRE BEVANDE *other beverages*

AN APERITIVO BEFORE DINNER teases the taste buds and gives us a moment to chat a bit before it's time to eat. Italians may meet first at a nice bar for an aperitivo and then go to the restaurant. Or they may eat some finger food that is laid at the front of the bar and, a few hours later, eat dinner at home.

There are two categories: *alcolici* and *analcolici*, alcoholic and nonalcoholic. Even when it contains alcohol, Italians prefer to drink something that is light and not too sweet.

Campari was created at Caffè Zucca in Milan in 1867. Zucca is located (though in a different location than the original) in the Galleria Vittorio Emanuele, which was built to celebrate the unification of Italy. The owner, Gaspare Campari, flavored the mixture with bitter herbs and orange zest. Serve cold with soda (*Americano*) or orange juice. *Negroni* is Campari, red vermouth, gin, ice, and orange or lemon peel. In a *Negroni sbagliato*, or "wrong" *Negroni*, gin was replaced with *spumante*.

Prosecco, the sparkling, easy drinking wine from Veneto, is also consumed as an aperitivo—or for a sweeter bubbly, try *spumante*. If prosecco is mixed with Aperol, a mild orange bitter, a few ice cubes, a slice of lemon, and perhaps a little soda, you'll have a Spritzer. It is fresh but still with that bitterness that is so loved in Italy. A Bellini is a blend of prosecco and white peach puree.

Cynar is a bitter liqueur made from artichokes. It is consumed both as an *aperitivo* and *digestivo*.

There are several major nonalcoholic brands, such as Crodino and Sanbittèr, with adult, bitter flavors.

AFTER DINNER, ITALIANS DRINK a *digestivo* to aid digestion. Often, it is a decoction similar to herb-based medicines. Like many liqueurs, these recipes often originated in the monasteries. These drinks are also called *amaro*, after the Italian word for bitter—a suitable description. Some *amari* are also used as a base in *aperitivi*. Popular brands: Amaro Averna, Fernet, Lucano Amaro, Ramazzotti.

Grappa, a brandy made from the grape residue from wine making, is also consumed as *digestivo*, as are aniseed-flavored Sambuca and the herb liqueur Strega.

Vermouth was invented in 1786 by Antonio Benedetto Carpano of Turin, Piedmont. The Martini family in Piedmont began production in 1863 and later merged with the manufacturer Rossi. Vermouth is consumed as an *aperitivo* or a *digestivo*, mixed in drinks, and used in cooking. Cinzano and Carpano Punt e Mes are other major Italian brands.

Limoncello is a lemon liqueur that is often served in Naples, along the Amalfi Coast, and in other places in Campania. It may only be called Limoncello if it comes from the Sorrento Peninsula, Capri, or the Amalfi Coast and is made with special lemons. The ones that are produced in other locations usually carry names like lemonello and limoncino. Lemon liqueurs are popular throughout southern Italy and in Sardinia and Sicily. They are often served straight from the freezer.

Limoncello

Lemon liqueur

Limoncello is also great to drizzle on top of fresh strawberries or other fruit, to flavor ice cream or sorbet, and to use in desserts. Organic lemons taste the best, especially if they are in season (in wintertime).

The number of lemons is hard to determine. It depends on how flavored they are. And the amount of alcohol and syrup is also determined by the lemon flavor. In other words, you need to play it by ear.

5 medium-sized, organic lemons
2 ½ cups (5 dl) neutral grain alcohol
14 oz (400 g) sugar
2 ½ cups (5 dl) water

Clean and dry the lemon. Cut the peels off of the lemons but avoid the white part, the pith, as it has a very bitter taste. Let the peels soak in the alcohol in a closed glass jar for two weeks.

Bring sugar and water to a boil. Stir so that the sugar dissolves. Let cool.

Filter the alcohol through a coffee filter. Throw the peels out.

Blend syrup and alcohol. Taste along the way and find a nice blend. It is ideal to store the limoncello in the freezer; it tastes the best if it is very cold.

CAFFÈ *coffee*

JUST LIKE WITH THE TOMATO, ITALIANS have adopted coffee and made it their own.

The first coffee brewers came in the 1800s. They were placed on the stove, just like the current angled Moka coffee brewers in aluminum. This is still the most common way for Italians to make coffee at home in the mornings. They drink coffee black or with a little milk.

At the end of the 1800s, the larger coffee brewers popped up at the bars. These machines could brew multiple cups in a row, but at times, you needed to release pressure, and the steam covered the bar.

These brewers could not only warm the milk for a caffè latte, but could also foam it—*cappuccino*. Because the machines were hard to handle, a proud new group of professionals were born: *barista* (which actually means bartender).

The modern espresso machine was first presented in 1946 by Achilles Gaggia. He had been developing it at his bar in Milan. The espresso with *crema*, the light brown foam on the top, was born. During the 1970s, the first mass-produced coffee brewers for use at home were made.

THE COFFEE IS ROASTED AND BLENDED to go with the espresso machines. The beans are ground right before they are brewed. For a perfect cup, the degree the coffee beans are ground and how hard the coffee is pressed need to be finely adjusted. Since the 1950s they have developed the technique of the four ms: *miscela* (blending), *macinazione* (grounding), *macchina* (machine), and *mano* (craft).

Traditionally, Italian espresso contained the simple and cheap bean *robusta* which yields a strong and slightly chocolate-flavored coffee with lots of *crema*. Nowadays the coffee is blended with the much nicer *arabica*.

In recent years, many new smaller breweries have appeared all over Italy by a younger and curious generation. Coffee is now getting more similar to wine when it comes to quality and roots.

Espresso is often consumed with sugar. When you order an espresso you simply say, *"Un caffè per favore."*

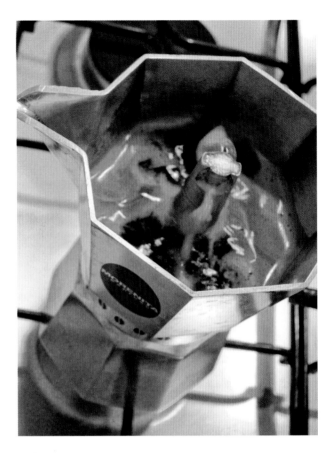

THE MOST COMMON COFFEE VARIETIES:

Caffè espresso—3 cl coffee from about 0.2 oz (7 grams) of finely ground coffee.

Caffè ristretto, caffè corto—As much coffee, less water.

Caffè lungo—More water.

Caffè Doppio—Double espresso.

Caffè romano—Some lemon.

Caffè corretto—Laced with spirits, corrected.

Cappuccino—With skimmed milk: Chiaro (light) with more milk, scuro (dark) with less milk. Only in the morning.

Caffè latte—Children's coffee. A lot of milk. Consumed in the morning.

Caffè Latte Macchiato—Even more milk.

Caffè macchiato—Espresso "stained" with a little milk.

Caffè con boiler—With whipped cream.

Caffè mocha—With hot chocolate.

Caffè freddo—Chilled espresso with sugar.

Shakerato—Cold espresso shaken with ice and sugar, served up without ice.

Frappe di caffè—Espresso, sugar, ice, and milk as a milkshake.

Caffè affogato—Espresso over ice cream.

ACQUA *water*

ITALIANS CONSUME THE MOST bottled water out of all of Europe—45 gallons (170 liters) per person per year in the south and 53 gallons (200 liters) in the north. This is twice as much as the European average (22 gallons (85 liters) and makes them the third largest consumer of bottled water in the world, despite the fact that many places have regular water, often from wells. But there is also a tradition of traveling to small wells in the district and filling plastic canisters.

Many wells that are now tapped commercially have been known for hundreds or even thousands of years. They are often a great source of income for the region they belong to.

Bottled water is a big business in Italy. There are about 600 different brands with different tastes and characters. The local patriotism also rules when it comes to water. Minerals and salt content are listed on all bottles. Water without bubbles is called *liscia* (flat), *non gassata*, or *naturale*. With bubbles: *gassate* or *frizzante*. *Leggermente gassata* is lightly carbonated. The carbon acid may be natural or added.

A FEW OF THE MOST POPULAR BRANDS OF WATER:

Levissima—Comes from the highest situated source in Bormio, Lombardy.

Ferrarelle—Riardo source, Emilia–Romagna.

Vera—from Veneto.

San Pellegrino—There was talk of this water's healing powers even in the 1200s. Val Brembana at Bergamo, Lombardy.

Uliveto—Slight natural carbonation; from Vico Pisano, Tuscany.

Rochetta—Low on minerals and carbonation; from Umbria.

Boiler—From Orvieto.

Fiucci—Health well in Lazio.

Lauretana—Ancient spring in Graglia in the Piedmontese Alps.

Santa Vittoria—From the Dolomites in Veneto.

Sole—From Lombardy.

San Benedetto—Ancient fountain in the Dolomites, Veneto.

LA DISPENSA *the pantry*

A brief overview of charcuterie, cheese, preserved foods, and other things you may like to eat.

Aceto balsamico—Balsamic vinegar. *Aceto Balsamico Tradizionale* is the finest. Viscous and stored for at least 12 years. There are also some that are stored four times as long. You only need to use a tiny bit. *Aceto Balsamico di Modena* is a very simple, regular balsamic vinegar, which is origin-labeled and whose production is to some extent controlled. All other balsamic are imitations, and quality and manufacturing methods vary.

Anchovies—A must in the pantry. Used as a flavor additive in many dishes. Rinse and dry before use.

Arborio—Creamy risotto rice; read more in risotto recipes.

Asiago—Half-fat cheese from cow's milk, Veneto. Actually two cheeses: *Asiago d'allevo*, a dessert, which is unseasoned and used as a cheese for grating when stored. And *Asiago pressato*, a hard cheese.

Baccalà—Salted, dried codfish, also known as *stoccafisso*.

Borlotti—Mild, pale brown beans.

Bottarga—Salted and dried roe of tuna, *tonno*, or gray mullet, *muggine*.

Bresaola—salted and air-dried beef. Dark brown and has a more intense flavor than prosciutto. From the Alps in Lombardy.

Cacciatore, cacciatorino—Sausage made from pork and sometimes beef. Coarsely ground. No larger than the hunter (*cacciatore*) can carry in his pocket. Air-dried, white mold on the skin, which is removed. Piedmont and Lombardy.

Caciocavallo—Pear-shaped cheese of sheep's or cow's milk. Originally from Sicily, now produced in the whole of Southern Italy. Reminiscent of aged provolone.

Cannellini—White beans from Tuscany.

Capperi—Capers. Green berries that are actually unopened flowers. The finest come from the island of Pantelleria off of Sicily.

Caprino—Italian goat cheese. *Capra* means goat, but most of the cheeses are made with a blend of goat and cow's milk, or solely cow's milk. Store in olive oil.

Carnaroli—The most expensive risotto rice with both creaminess and firm consistency. Read more in risotto recipes.

Casalinga—Means homemade. The name refers to a salami, which is thicker and has a strong taste.

Cinghiale—Wild boar.

Coppa—Rolled loin of pork that is salted, dried, and aged. The skin is not eaten.

Culatello di Zibello—The finest top of the ham. Salted and air-dried. Emilia–Romagna.

Cuscusu—Couscous. Common in Sicily.

Finocchiona—Fennel-flavored salami from Tuscany, among others places.

Fior di latte—The actual name of the mozzarella made of cow's milk. Originally used for *insalata caprese* as *fior di latte* is produced in nearby Sorrento.

Fontina—Semi soft, fat cow's milk cheese from Val d'Aosta in the Alps. Very mild.

Gorgonzola—Blue cheese, originally from the village of the same name near Milan, Lombardy. Over 1,000-year-old tradition.

Grana Padano—Hard cheese from Lombardy of cow's milk; similar to Parmesan, but produced under less stringent requirements. Somewhat milder.

Guanciale—Salted and cured pork cheek. Much appreciated in Rome. Pancetta substitute.

Lardo—Lard, i.e., white fat from pork that is dry-salted, dried, smoked, or soaked in wine. Seasoned with rosemary and other herbs. For example, *Lardo di Colonnata* from Tuscany. Natural *lardo* is used in cooking and the flavored kind is served as an antipasto.

Marsala—Sicilian fortified wine from the town of the same name. Looks like port and sherry. Can be dry, medium dry, or sweet—*secco, semisecco,* or *dolce.*

Mascarpone—Soft, creamy, semi-runny cheese from Lombardy. Like a mild sour cream.

Mortadella—Giant sausage from Bologna. Mild, lean, and smooth, often with pistachio nuts. Manufactured in many places.

Mostarda—*Mostarda di frutta,* fruit steeped in a syrup of sugar, vinegar, and mustard powder.

Mozzarella di bufala Campana—the real mozzarella. Made from buffalo milk mainly from the plains south of Salerno, Campania. Cow's milk mozzarella's real name is *fior di latte.*

'Nduja—Spicy salami from Calabria. Soft and spreadable.

Pancetta—Pork, salted, flavored, and air-dried, usually unsmoked but may also be found smoked, *affumicata.* Similar to bacon, but bacon contains water.

Parma ham—See *prosciutto di Parma.*

Parmesan—See *parmigiano reggiano.*

Parmigiano reggiano—Parmesan cheese, the only cheese made from cow's milk from Emilia–Romagna. The production of *parmigiano reggiano* is strictly regulated when it co-mes to which milk is used and where and how it may be made.

Passata—Anything strained. Often this referes to *passata di pomodoro,* strained tomatoes that are mostly sold in bottles.

Paste—Biscuits and small cakes from the bakery, *la pasticceria.*

Pecorino—Sheep's milk cheese. *Pecora* means sheep. Various types of pecorino are produced in Central and Southern Italy. Available fresh and aged. From mild to strong. The stored, aged cheese hardens faster than Parmesan and is therefore cheaper. It is used in the same manner. *Pecorino Romano* may now be produced in Sardinia and was made as early as the first century after Christ. It is a little peppery. *Pecorino sardo* (Sardinia) may be mild or a little sharper. *Pecorino siciliano* is mentioned in ancient Greek texts, and *pecorino toscano* dates back to the Etruscans. Pecorino cheese is more common than Parmesan in the South.

Peperoncino—Hot pepper. Fresh or dried. Small ones are dried whole, *interi,* or broken into flakes (sometimes called chili flakes here at home), *frantumato,* which is often used. The whole peperoncino is easier to remove when the dish is spicy enough.

Pine nuts—*Pinoli,* actually a seed from cones of the pine tree.

Polenta—Coarsely ground corn flour. See p. 90.

Porcini—Ceps.

Prosciutto cotto—Cooked ham.

Prosciutto crudo—Cured ham, for instance, Parma ham or *San Daniele.*

Prosciutto di San Daniele—Cured ham from Friuli–Venezia Giulia. Milder than prosciutto.

Prosciutto di Parma—Salted and cured ham, *prosciutto crudo*, from Parma, Emilia–Romagna. 2000-year-old traditions. Mild. Strictly controlled manufacturing. Matures for at least one year and up to 30 months.

Prosciutto toscano—Regulated, air-dried ham from Tuscany. Seasoned with salt, black pepper, and herbs.

Provola affumicata—Reminiscent of mozzarella cheese. Hard cheese. Smoked.

Provolone—Semi-hard cheese from cow's milk originally from the South. Many shapes and flavors from mild to piquant, *dolce* to *piccante*. Fresh or aged.

Radicchio—Red bitter salad, lettuce rose, or rose salad that is not really a salad but a relative of the endive. Round from Verona. Oblong like the endive or long curled leaves from Treviso.

Ricotta—Whey from mozzarella production is cooked and becomes ricotta. Cream cheese. *Ricotta salata* is salted and aged and broken or torn, almost like feta cheese. Ricotta is made of cow's, buffalo's, and sheep's milk.

Robiola di Roccaverano—Fatty cream cheese of cow's and goat's or sheep's milk, Piedmont.

Rocket, ruchetta, rughetta—Different names for rocket, also known as arugula. *Rucola selvatica* is wild arugula.

Salame Cinta Senese—From Tuscany; made from Cinta Senese pork.

Salame di Cinghiale—Wild boar salami. Common in Tuscany.

Salame di Felino—Medium, rough, mild salami from Parma. Black pepper, garlic, and white wine. The same pork as the Parma ham.

Salame di Milano—Finely ground pork and beef. Matures for a few months. Mild.

Salame di Napoli—Coarsely ground and seasoned with black pepper, garlic, piri-piri, and white wine. Smoked and stored.

Salame di tartufo bianco—Flavored with real white truffles.

Salame soppressata—Air-dried, pressed salami with black pepper and garlic. Common in Veneto. *Soppressata* from Calabria is very flavorful with garlic, peppers, and peperoncino.

Salame toscano—Mild salami marinated in red wine.

Salsiccia—Fresh sausage ranging from mild to strong. Seasoned with garlic, fennel, truffle, and wine.

Salsiccia di Calabria—Salami from Calabria with peperoncino and fennel.

Salsiccia Napoletana piccante—Air-dried, spicy, and lightly smoked salami from Naples.

Scamorza—Reminiscent of mozzarella and sometimes used as a substitute. Hard cheese. Also available smoked, *affumicata*.

Semolina—Durum wheat flour.

Speck—Air-dried and smoked pork from the north; almost bacon.

Stoccafisso—Dried fish, usually cod.

Taleggio—Cheese made from cow's milk. From the Alps, with ancient roots. Matures and becomes soft in the middle. The brine gives a reddish crust you can eat.

Toma piemontese—Soft, gentle cheese made from cow's milk. Originated in Roman times. Stronger if aged. Other tomato cheeses are made with both sheep and goat's milk.

Ventricina—Hot salami from Abruzzo and Campania.

Vialone—Risotto with a firmer texture than arborio. Read more in the risotto recipes.

Vin santo—Amber-colored dessert wine originally from Tuscany.

MUSICA PER CUCINARE
music for cooking

Yearlong research in our kitchen has found that the food turns out better if we play Italian music. Here is some music that has a confirmed positive effect on the food (not to mention the fact that the cooking becomes that much more fun!).

Many Italian artists are also famous in the Latin world, including South America, and they record their records in Spanish as well. Make sure that you get the Italian original when you order music online. (Studies have shown that the food just doesn't turn out as good with the Spanish versions.)

It is remarkable how many of these artists had their breakthroughs at the annual San Remo Festival. It's like a Eurovision Song Contest, but much larger and more important. Everyone plays at the San Remo festival! And famous artists gladly return there. In addition to these albums, we usually listen to Italian radio via the Internet, mainly RAI Uno. It is also good for cooking.

Laura Pausini—Born 1974 in Faenza, Emilia–Romagna, she was a wunderkind and gained a more mature voice with time. On the early records, she was already a good singer but tended to overdo it a bit. She had her breakthrough at the San Remo Festival in 1993 with "La solitudine." Classic Italian melodic pop, romantic, preferably ballads, often magnificent. A greatest hits collection is a good start.

A selection of records: *Laura Pausini* (1993), *Laura* (1994), *Le cose che vivi* (1996), *La mia risposta* (1998), *Tra te e il mare* (2000), *Resta in ascolto* (2004), *Io Canto* (2006), *Primavera in anticipo* (2008).

Eros Ramazzotti—Born in 1963 in Rome. He had his breakthrough at the San Remo Festival in 1984 with "Terra promessa." He has returned several times to the festival. Classic Italian melodic pop and slightly radio pop, often with pumping bass. Romantic, often ballads. Has made more mature music in later years and is good at both guitar and piano. Successful also outside of Italy. A greatest hits collection is a good start.

A selection of records: *In certi momenti* (1987), *Musica è* (1988), *In ogni senso* (1990), *Tutte storie* (1993), *Dove c'è musica* (1996), *stilelibero* (2000), *Calma apparente* (2005), *9* (2003), *Ali e radici* (2009).

Pino Daniele—Born in 1955 in Naples, Campania. With roots in traditional Neapolitan music, he was influenced by rock and blues from the 1960s and 1970s. Calls his own music *taramblù*, after tarantula, rhumba, and blues. Strong Arabic and Latin influences. Often sings in Neapolitan. Very popular in southern Italy. Melodic, often quiet, smooth, a little jazzy. Incredibly awesome to hear a live audience sing along to the quiet songs. The collection *Napule è* is a good introduction.

His best known songs: "Quando," "Napule è," "'O scarrafone." Albums: *Terra mia* (1977), *Daniele Pino* (1979), *E sona mo'* (live, 1993), *Medina* (2001), *Passi D'Autore* (2004), *Iguana cafè* (2005).

Arisa—Born in 1982 in Genoa, Liguria, but moved weeks after birth to Pignola, Basilicata, where her family is from. Her real name is Rosalba Pippa. Had her breakthrough at the San Remo Festival in 2009 with "Sincerità," also the name of her first album. Naive, bubbly, and happy music. Music: "Sincerità," "Malamorenò."

Carmen Consoli—Born in 1979 in Catania, Sicily. Had her breakthrough at San Remo 1996. Rock and blues is her foundation. African and Arabic influences. Beautiful, sad, and at times dark. Album: *Eva contro Eva* (2006).

Fiordaliso—Fiordaliso is her surname and stage name; Marina is her first name. Born in 1956 in Piacenza, Emilia–Romagna. San Remo in 1982. Pop rock with a rough appearance in the Italian style, which for women means a little hoarse and slightly dangerous voice—very popular and common in Italy. Album: *Il portico di Dio* (1991).

Fred Buscaglione—Name was really Ferdinando. Born 1921 in Turin, Piedmont. Died in Rome in 1960. Singer and actor who was big in the 1950s. Typical music of the period. Strong US influence. Pretend dangerous and pretend tough. Famous songs: "Che bambola," "Guarda che luna," "Love in Portofino." Died when his pink Ford Thunderbird collided with a truck in the early morning hours outside the US Embassy in Rome. Top: *Il Favoloso Fred Buscaglione*.

Giorgia—Last name is Todrani. Born in 1971 in Rome, Lazio. Vocal virtuoso who can compete with early Whitney

Houston and Mariah Carey. Italian R & B and soul, which becomes a little more melodic and pop-ish. Very famous in Italy. Debuted at San Remo in 1994 with one of her biggest hits: "E poi." Has sung with Luciano Pavarotti, Pino Daniele, Ray Charles, Ronan Keating, Herbie Hancock, and Elton John. Should make more records. Album: *Greatest Hits, le cose non vanno mai come credi* (2002).

Irene Grandi—Born in 1969 in Florence, Tuscany. Had breakthrough at San Remo in 1994, the same year as Andrea Bocelli. Also has a somewhat dangerously hoarse voice, but not as theatrically exaggerated as in many others. Firmly rooted in pop and rock history, with nice melodies. Her records are very spaced out, but always very good. Took part in San Remo as late as 2010. Albums: *Irene Grandi* (1994), *Prima di partire* (2003), *Indelebile* (2005), *Alle porte del sogno* (2010).

Nek—Real name Filippo Neviani. Born in 1972 in Sassuolo, Emilia–Romagna. Did his first album in 1992, and San Remo the year after. Had a huge hit with the song "Laura non c'è" at San Remo in 1997. Reminiscent of Eros Ramazzotti musically. Modern, rhythmic, and ballad-like melodies. Has done well outside of Italy. Albums: *Lei, gli amici e tutto il resto* (1997), *La vita è* (2000), *Le cose da difendere* (2002), *Una parte di me* (2005), *Nella stanza 26* (2006).

Pacifico—Real name Gino de Crescenzo, born in 1964 in Milan, Lombardy. Mom and Dad were from Campania. University graduate who studied economics and political science. From this artist comes dreamy, soaring, cinematic music. San Remo 2004. Albums: *Dentro ogni casa* (2009).

Renato Carosone—Born in 1920 in Naples, Campania, died in 2001 in Rome. One of the greatest names in Italian popular music of the second half of the 1900s. Educated at the conservatory. His music mixes traditional Neapolitan songs with jazz, swing, 1950s pop, and 1960s pop. Mad, fun, and a classic in Italy. Typical music of 1950s and 1960s Italy. San Remo. Famous songs: "Tu vuò fá l'americano," "O sarracino," "Maruzzella," "Mambo italian." Albums: collections such as *I piu grand: successi di Renato Carosone* (1996).

Tiziano Ferro—Born 1980 in Latina, Lazio. First appearance in San Remo in 1997 was not very good. San Remo 1998, on the other hand, was when he was discovered. Rap meets Italian pop hits with a distinctive voice. Suggestive. Has sold more than 8 million albums. Also great in Spanish. Albums: *Nessuno è solo* (2006), *All mia etá* (2008).

Collection of pop hits from the 1950s and 1960s are always a good help when cooking. For instance: *Nostalgia italiana 1963* (with light Paul Anka and Neil Sedaka as well), *Viva Italia! Festive Italian Classic*s (with, among others, Sophia Loren and Perry Como).

Luciano Pavarotti—Born in 1935 in Modena, Emilia–Romagna; died in Modena in 2007. Introduction is not really necessary. When he was at his best, he was divine. Our children call it pasta music, but it works with all dishes.

Opera's greatest hits and Neapolitan songs.

Records: *Tutto Pavarotti* (1989) is a good collection of the opera and Neapolitan songs; *O Sole Mio!* (1990), with only songs; *Passione* (1990), more Neapolitan songs; *Three tenors in concert* (1990), filmed concerts outdoors in Rome with Plácido Domingo and José Carreras.

Giacomo Puccini—*Puccini Gold* (2008), a collection of opera's greatest hits—in other words, the masterpieces of Puccini. With Luciano Pavarotti, Plácido Domingo, Andrea Bocelli, Renee Fleming, Jose Carreras, Montserrat Caballé.

Jussi Björling—A collection of Jussi's greatest is also a must. Still remembered and popular in Italy. For instance: *The king of tenors* (1999) by Verdi and Puccini.

Andrea Bocelli—You can get in the Christmas mood year-round with *Sacred Arias* (1999). Beautiful as your Italian cathedral of choice.

INDEX